Prayers
for
HOPE and COMFORT

Prayers
for
HOPE and COMFORT

*Reflections, Meditations,
and Inspirations*

MAGGIE OMAN SHANNON

Conari Press

First published in 2008 by Conari Press,
an imprint of Red Wheel/Weiser, LLC
With offices at:
500 Third Street, Suite 230
San Francisco, CA 94107
www.redwheelweiser.com

ISBN: 978-1-57324-319-3
Library of Congress Cataloging-in-Publication Data is avail-
able upon request.

Cover and text design by Donna Linden
Typeset in Futura, Garamond, and Handsome
Cover photograph © Philip Harvey/Corbis

Printed in Canada
TCP
10 9 8 7 6 5 4 3 2 1

The paper used in this publication meets the minimum
requirements of the American National Standard for
Information Sciences—Permanence of Paper for Printed
Library Materials Z39.48-1992 (R1997).

Dedicated with deepest love
to my precious daughter,
Chloe Xin Shannon,
who graces each day—
even the ones that feel hard—
with everything that is bright and beautiful

and to all the children of our world

Contents

Introduction

Some say that "there are no accidents"; and if that is true, then it's not surprising that I would be working on *Prayers for Hope and Comfort* during one of the hardest times in my own life. Thankfully, I faced nothing severe or shocking—just a period in which challenges in almost every arena of my life converged at exactly the same time: sudden and unexpected responsibilities in my workplace; the requirements of a weekend graduate program; the looming deadline of this book; the daily demands of rearing a three-year-old; a marriage in low ebb because it kept getting relegated to the "back burner"; the saddening need for increased involvement in my mother's medical matters due to dementia associated with Parkinson's disease; and, because I wasn't taking care of myself, my own minor but lingering health issues. Though I remained acutely aware that many, many people face situations like this or indeed much worse, still, the collective weight of what I was juggling frequently felt overwhelming.

As a trained spiritual director, I have witnessed how God speaks to us in and through the circumstances of our lives; and as I worked on this project I tried to notice how I was handling this particular hard time of my own, how I was—and wasn't—reaching out to God. To tell the truth, I found it hard to pray during this period—I was too caught up in the erroneous sense that I didn't have time to pray, that I had to make use of every spare moment for the seemingly endless array of things on my "to do" list. Sometimes it seemed that if I stopped to feel all the emotions I was so carefully erecting fences around, I wouldn't be able to complete what needed to be done on any given day. Mixed in with the daily pedestrian concerns about taking the car in to the repair shop, or the cat in to the vet, my heart—stretched by a growing sense of social justice and a deep desire to be of service—longed also to be addressing far larger concerns about the world.

When I had no choice, when those little structures that we erect to keep ourselves going started cracking, I did stop. And in the stillness I realized anew that comfort, renewal, and deep peace can always be found in the present moment, if we allow ourselves even a few minutes to rest with our Source. No matter what the circumstances of our lives are, we can place ourselves in the presence of the Divine the moment we decide to be still, to breathe, to release our worries and our heartbreaks to God, to ease ourselves gently into the silence of the Sacred.

I also found great inspiration in these pieces that you are about to read, and believe that you will, too; they demonstrate how deeply the written words of others, expressed with a fierce authenticity born of pain, can touch us to the core. Here, you will find the words of men, women, and children from around the world and throughout the ages as they address the Spirit of their understanding—prayers that, though they may be written in noninclusive language that reflects the historical period in which they wrote them, remain resonant expressions of the heart. Because these authentic, and very human, passages are so powerful, I made the decision not to include a large number of passages from any faith's scriptures, believing that more power can reside in an original voice grappling with pain and unknowing than in a codified, and perhaps well-known, scriptural passage.

It has been made very clear to me that we do need to come from a place of renewal and groundedness ourselves before we can truly be of service to another; and I have always found great comfort and beauty in the awareness that we each have the opportunity to become alchemists with our pain—to transmute our own sufferings into something golden when we can offer that great gift of empathy, and the greater gift of compassionate action, to another who is experiencing a painful life situation. Therefore, you will see a clear bias in the choice of selections, a bias toward hope and healing. Developing this project, whose working title was *Prayers for Hard Times,* I didn't think it would be helpful only to have a collection of lamentations. It seemed increasingly important that this book contain wisdom, that it point to things that would give its readers faith and inspiration, and ultimately that it contain a vision— even a call—with which to move into our fragile future. For as Helen Keller wrote, "Although the world is full of suffering, it is full also of the overcoming of it."

Therefore, this book is organized into five sections, representing the concentric circles of compassion that extend naturally as we heal and grow spiritually. First, there are prayers for ourselves, as we each always begin there; it is difficult to focus on another's suffering when we ourselves are in pain. Then, as we begin to look outside of ourselves, come prayers for our relationships—parents, children, partners, friends, pets, colleagues—followed by prayers for our community and for our world. The final section contains prayers for our planet, words devoted to seeing oneness not only among all peoples, but among all beings in this great web of life.

While working on this book, I created a little shrine under my computer monitor with elements no more than five inches high: a Peruvian clay figurine of a girl praying; a crystal Quan Yin, hearer of the world's cries; a small metal Ganesh, destroyer of obstacles; a raku heart rattle, transformed by fire into a musical instrument; a prayer locket containing this tiny printed prayer: "May the footprints of the Lord lead me in times of strife"; a depiction of Jesus, illustrating his example of compassion-in-action; and a candle imprinted with the word *hope*. Whatever prayer means to you personally, it is my prayer that you will find selections here that reflect your cries, destroy your obstacles, transform your fires into music, lead you in times of strife, compel you to action, and most of all, give you hope.

Maggie Oman Shannon
San Francisco, California

Prayers
for
Ourselves

When your eyes are tired
the world is tired also.

When your vision has gone
no part of the world can find you.

Time to go into the dark
where the night has eyes
to recognize its own.

There you can be sure
you are not beyond love.

The dark will be your home
   tonight.

The night will give you a horizon
further than you can see.

You must learn one thing.
The world was made to be free in.

Give up all the other worlds
except the one to which you belong.

Sometimes it takes darkness and the sweet
confinement of your aloneness
to learn

anything or anyone
that does not bring you alive

is too small for you.
　　　—David Whyte, "Sweet Darkness"

If a man wishes to be sure of the road he treads on,
he must close his eyes and walk in the dark.
　　　—Saint John of the Cross

O Great Spirit,
Whose voice I hear in the winds,
and whose breath gives life to all the world,
hear me! I am small and weak, I need your
strength and wisdom.
Let me walk in Beauty, and make my eyes
ever behold the red and purple sunset.

Make my hands respect the things you have
made and my ears sharp to hear your voice.

Make me wise so that I may understand the
things you have taught my people.

Let me learn the lessons you have hidden
in every leaf and rock.

I seek strength, not to be greater than my
brother, but to fight my greatest enemy—myself.

Make me always ready to come to you with
clean hands and straight eyes.

So when life fades, as the fading sunset,
my spirit may come to you without shame.
    —Native American prayer

Give me, O Lord, a steadfast heart, which no unworthy affection may drag downwards; give me an unconquered heart, which no tribulation can wear out; give me an upright heart, which no unworthy purpose may tempt aside.

Bestow on me also, O Lord my God, understanding to know Thee, diligence to seek Thee, wisdom to find Thee, and a faithfulness that may finally embrace Thee. Amen.

—Saint Thomas Aquinas

A pain in the mind is the prelude to all discovery.

—Sir Almroth Wright

The love of God enfolds me
The love of God surrounds me
The love of God saturates me
The love of God upholds me
The love of God strengthens me
The love of God comforts me
The love of God cheers me
The love of God restores me

The love of God calms me
The love of God consoles me
The love of God guides me
The love of God protects me
The love of God cleanses me
The love of God frees me
The love of God fulfills me
The love of God heals me
The love of God uplifts me
The love of God embraces me
The love of God envelopes me
The love of God fills me
The love of God shines in me
and eternally sustains me

—Magdolene Mogyorosi, "The Love of God"

You gain strength, courage and confidence by every experience in which you really stop to look fear in the face. You are able to say to yourself, "I have lived through this horror. I can take the next thing that comes along." You must do the thing you think you cannot do.

—Eleanor Roosevelt

When some great sorrow like a mighty river
Flows through your life with peace-destroying
    power,
And the dearest things are swept from sight forever,
Say to yourself each trying hour,
"This too will pass away."

    —Author unknown

Suffering is a device to turn one's thoughts in the
direction of God.

    —Sufi saying

I sit on my butt in the dark
Back against the cliff,
Dazed and shaken.
Who knew that I could fall so far?
I was only trying to make my life
A reflection of the dreams
You keep offering.
No one mentioned the cost.
No one told me there was Danger
On the road less traveled.

The Void is a terrible thing.
But if I am to prosper on my Path, I must go
    there.
Muddled and shaken, I feel abandoned and alone.
There in the misty Darkness,
I flail about until exhaustion overcomes me.
What should I do next?
What *should* I do next?
Whimpering, I allow the silence to engulf me.
I lie there as one separated from her very soul.

And in the silence, a still, small voice whispers . . .

Get up? Get up, you say?
Am I to have *no* mercy?
Oh.
Okay, then . . .

Giving thanks, I step into my future.
Blessed be the path before me.
Blessed be Your Many Names.
Blessed, Blessed be.

I must be off now . . .
    —Anne Keeler Evans, "A Prayer for Falling"

13

God always answers us in the deeps, never in the
shallows of our souls.

—Amy Carmichael

O Merciful God, who answerest the poor,
   Answer us,
O Merciful God, who answerest the lowly in spirit,
   Answer us,
O Merciful God, who answerest the broken of
         heart,
   Answer us.
O Merciful God,
   Answer us.
O Merciful God,
   Have compassion.
O Merciful God,
   Redeem.
O Merciful God,
   Save.
O Merciful God, have pity upon us,
   Now,
   Speedily,
   And at a near time.
      —Jewish prayer for the Day of Atonement

Each day I pray: God give me strength anew
To do the task I do not wish to do,
To measure what I am by what I give—
God give me strength that I may rightly live.
   —Author unknown

Lead, kindly Light, amid the encircling gloom,
   Lead Thou me on;
The night is dark, and I am far from home,
   Lead Thou me on;
Keep Thou my feet. I do not ask to see
The distant scene; one step's enough for me.

I was not ever thus, nor prayed that Thou
   Shouldst lead me on;
I loved to choose and see my path, but now
   Lead Thou me on;
I loved the garish day, and, spite of fears,
Pride ruled my will. Remember not past years.

So long Thy power hath blessed me; sure it still
   Will lead me on

O'er moor and fen, o'er crag and torrent, till
    The night is gone;
And with the morn those angel faces smile,
Which I have loved long since and lost awhile.
    —John Henry Newman

When you are full of problems, there is no room for anything new to enter, no room for a solution. So whenever you can, make some room, create some space, so that you find the life underneath your life situation.
    —Eckhart Tolle

Lord God,
I am begging you
It's me, [name]
I'm begging you
I'm begging you to take my hand
Lift me up, out of darkness
Into the light
Lift me out of my addiction.

Lord God,
Take my hand
It's me, [name]
Begging you to take my hand
Just for today
Lift me up into the light of your love
So that I may see
The reflection of my face in yours.

Restore me to sanity.
Fill me with your grace.
Amen.

—Molly Starr, "A Prayer for the Hardest of Times"

God is in every experience of the world. For those
who fear the impossibility of such things, there
is always one way through their tunnel. It is to
believe that it is a tunnel. That there is a light at the
end. That it is worth waiting, that it is wise
to be open to all new ideas, all new impressions.

—Anne Shells

In the stillness of the morning
I meet you in my prayer.
Your presence like an incense,
Fragrance everywhere.

Come Sophia Wisdom,
With your holy light.
Come Sophia Wisdom
Make the darkness bright.

You're there within the story
That whispers through the trees
Of promise, play and passion
Dancing in the breeze.

O ever present Mystery!
O ever Ancient Bond!
You hold us in the Spiral
Which carries us beyond.

—Diane Forrest, OP, "Sophia Wisdom"

Every day can't be a good day.
But within each day—those
long twenty-four hours—there
are a few minutes or even

seconds when something good
or special happens.

Those moments are as powerful
as the frail flame of a candle
that can light an entire dark room.
  —Judith Garrett Garrison and Scott Sheperd

February is neither here nor there.
Not holiday.
Not beginning of school year,
Nor New Year.
Not end.
Not ever,
"Finally! February is here!"
Never.

February just is.
It's a Tuesday kind of month.
A 10:15 in the morning kind of time
On a Tuesday
When one is 43.
Not 21.
Not 40.
Not celebratory.
Not married.

Not even engaged.
Not expecting a baby or a raise.
No deadlines looming.
No bulbs blooming yet.
Kind of wet,
An intermittent showers kind of time,
A chance of rain.

Not a chance of winning the lottery.
Not a chance of an unexpected trip to Spain.
No, just an "is" kind of time,
A just plain "is" kind of time,
Just plain.

And I wonder . . .

Because it *is* February
And there's time to wonder,
Because not tilling or sowing
Or weeding or reaping,
Just enough of sleeping and getting up
And working and going to bed,
To not be reading,
To not be well read,

  . . . how February fits
Into the scheme of things
And how I fit into the scheme of it.

So think of that Great Schemer,
Our Dear Redeemer
And wonder . . .

. . . what did Jesus do in February?

The February before being
In the temple at thirteen.
The February before Canaan.
The February before Golgotha.
Or the February after for that matter,
Floating like a specter forever
Over all of us he loves.
What did Jesus do in February?

And it occurs
That maybe that was when He went to the desert.
He surely couldn't have lasted forty days in July.
Even a Son of God couldn't bear these mortal bones
Over the sandy exile of July.

And suddenly I cry,
Watching the rain falling methodic from the sky,
Adding to the gray lapping of the Bay.
For somehow I know that February is the desert
    and my job
To be busy avoiding temptation

And remembering why
I listen to the voice of God in the fog
And am stronger for it somehow in July.

    —Ann Kyle-Brown, "February"

In these dark waters
Drawn up from my frozen well . . .
Glittering of spring

    —Ringai

Holy Spirit, Spirit of the Living God,
you breathe in us
on all that is inadequate and fragile,
You make living water spring even
from our hurts themselves.
And through you, the valley of tears
becomes a place of wellsprings.
So, in an inner life
with neither beginning nor end,
your continual presence
makes new freshness break through. Amen.

    —Brother Roger of Taize

The Lord is my Shepherd—
That's relationship!
I shall not want—
That's rest!
He leadeth me beside still waters—
That's refreshment!
He restoreth my soul—
That's healing!
He leadeth me in the paths of righteousness—
That's guidance!
For His name's sake—
That's purpose!
Yea, though I walk through the valley
of the shadow of death, I will fear no evil—
That's protection!
For thou art with me—
That's faithfulness!
Thy rod and thy staff they comfort me—
That's comfort!
Thou preparest a table before me
in the presence of mine enemies—
That's hope!
Thou anointest my head with oil—
That's consecration!
My cup runneth over—
That's abundance!
Surely goodness and mercy shall follow me

All the days of my life—
That's blessing!
And I will dwell in the house of the Lord—
That's security!
Forever—
That's eternity!

—Author unknown, adapted from Psalm 23

My personal trials have also taught me the value of
unmerited suffering. As my sufferings mounted I
soon realized that there were two ways that I could
respond to my situation: either to react with bitterness or to transform the suffering into a creative
force.

—Martin Luther King Jr.

"Make of yourself a light,"
said the Buddha,
before he died.
I think of this every morning
as the east begins
to tear off its many clouds
of darkness, to send up the first

signal—a white fan
streaked with pink and violet,
even green.
An old man, he lay down
between two sala trees,
and he might have said anything,
knowing it was his final hour.
The light burns upward,
it thickens and settles over the fields.
Around him, the villagers gathered
and stretched forward to listen.
Even before the sun itself
hangs, disattached, in the blue air,
I am touched everywhere
by its ocean of yellow waves.
No doubt he thought of everything
that had happened in his difficult life.
And then I feel the sun itself
as it blazes over the hills,
like a million flowers on fire—
clearly I'm not needed,
yet I feel myself turning
into something of inexplicable value.
Slowly, beneath the branches,
he raised his head.
He looked into the faces of that frightened crowd.

    —Mary Oliver, "The Buddha's Last Instruction"

And this is important to remember: given the fact of pain as a normal part of the experience of life, one may make the pain contribute to the soul, to the life meaning. One may be embittered, ground down by it, but one need not be. The pain of life may teach us to understand life and, in our understanding of life, to love life. To love life truly is to be whole in all one's parts; and to be whole in all one's parts is to be free and unafraid.

—Howard Thurman

Father-Mother, Teacher, Friend
    Great Spirit, God; Provider and Protector
This prayer I say for I need direction, hope, and strength:

My pain and my joy are beyond comprehension
I turn *everything* over to you
All judgments I release
Emptying the thoughts of craving, fear, dislike
I know the light can then be free to shine
Your light, my light, our light

Thank you for the Life that is my journey
Let me be *entirely* changed, so that only clear Being
    remains.
    —Wendy Wolters

Let mystery have its place in you; do not be always
turning up your whole soil with the plowshare of
self-examination, but leave a little fallow corner
in your heart ready for any seed the winds may
bring. . . . Keep a place in your heart for the unexpected guests, an altar for the unknown God.
    —Henri Frederic Amiel

Come, Lord,
and cover me with the night.
Spread your grace over us
as you assured us you would do.

Your promises are more than
all the stars in the sky;
your mercy is deeper than the night.
Lord, it will be cold.
The night comes with its breath of death.
Night comes; the end comes; you come.

Lord, we wait for you
day and night.
   —African prayer

There are as many nights as days, and the one is
just as long as the other in the year's course. Even a
happy life cannot be without a measure of darkness,
and the word "happy" would lose its meaning if it
were not balanced by sadness.
   —Carl Jung

Glimmer in me sweet
Help me dive deep
Protecting myself from swells of emotion,
Despair's stolen my thirst
All I feel is numb
So buffered from life I have become.

Divine in me
Fortitude, fearlessness
to drown more freely
(albeit temporarily)
Help me again find thirst

And know what it is
to be submerged,
ego lost
Old Being, dissolved.

I could pray for taking away
All my pain and angst-ridden days
Instead I ask
To newly bask
Giving up my All to
drown my woes
To bathe your sacred waters
To enter your wily whirlpool.

Oh, Sacred Endarkenment
Sacred Confusion
Fear of all fears
Help me discern the
Healing beauty Within your
Difficult Teachings.
Within your endarkening gifts, mysteriously
    disguised
I seek to Trust.

Hold me
Encompass me
Envelop my fragile shell

In your ever-flowing
Heart.
For my shell feels about to break, and
I know not who I will become
On the other side
Of transformation.

Help me to hold preciously
Seeds of doubt,
Seeds of fear.
Grace me with trust to Believe
I will again rebirth into Faith
With Hope to feel
deep watery fresh
thirst for Life
once again.

—Catherine Cameron, "Endarkenment Envelop Me"

Just as a mother would not love a child better for
its being turned into a model of perfection . . . but
does love it the more deeply every time it tries to
be good, so I do hope and believe our great Father
does not wait for us to be good and wise to love us,
but loves us, and loves to help us in the very thick
of our struggle.

—Juliana Horatia Ewing

Learn to wait—life's hardest lesson
    Conned, perchance, through blinding tears;
While the heart throbs sadly echo
    To the tread of passing years.
Learn to wait—hope's slow fruition;
    Faint not, though the way seems long;
There is joy in each condition;
    Hearts through suffering may grow strong.
    —Author unknown

Christianity has been reproached for trying to
deceive people about the reality of earthly suffering
by comforting them with the prospect of heavenly
blessedness awaiting them. Jesus was not thinking
of vague future bliss. For he does not say: Blessed
eventually will be those who now suffer. Rather he
promises: Blessed are you now, right this minute,
while you are suffering.
    —Albert Schweitzer

Much of our understanding of God's action in our lives is achieved in hindsight. When a particular crisis or event in our life has passed we cry out in astonishment like Jacob, "The Lord is in this place and I never knew it."

—Sheila Cassidy

Almighty God, the Father of mercies and God of all comfort, come to my help and deliver me from this difficulty that besets me. I believe Lord, that all trials of life are under Your care and that all things work for the good of those who love You. Take away from me fear, anxiety and distress. Help me to face and endure my difficulty with faith, courage and wisdom. Grant that this trial may bring me closer to You for You are my rock and refuge, my comfort and hope, my delight and joy. I trust in Your love and compassion. Blessed is Your name, Father, Son and Holy Spirit, now and forever. Amen.

—Orthodox prayer

Some of your griefs you have cured,
And the sharpest you will have survived;

But what torments of pain you endured
From the evils that never arrived!
 —Old French verse

It comes the very moment you wake up each morning. All your wishes and hopes for the day rush at you like wild animals. And the first job each morning consists simply in shoving them all back; in listening to that other voice, taking that other point of view, letting that other, larger, stronger, quieter life come flowing in. And so on, all day. Standing back from your natural fussings and frettings; coming in out of the wind.
 —C. S. Lewis

O God, let me not turn coward before the difficulties of the day or prove recreant to its duties. Let me not lose faith in my fellow men. Keep me sweet and sound of heart, in spite of ingratitude, treachery, or meanness. Preserve me from minding little stings or giving them. Amen.
 —Author unknown

There are so many gifts
Still unopened from your birthday,
There are so many hand-crafted presents
That have been sent to you by God.

The Beloved does not mind repeating,
"Everything I have is also yours."

Please forgive Hafiz and the Friend
If we break into a sweet laughter
When your heart complains of being thirsty
When ages ago
Every cell in your soul
Capsized forever
Into this infinite golden sea.

Indeed,
A lover's pain is like holding one's breath
Too long
In the middle of a vital performance,

In the middle of one of Creation's favorite
Songs.

Indeed, a lover's pain is this sleeping,
This sleeping,
When God just rolled over and gave you
Such a big good-morning kiss!

There are so many gifts, my dear,
Still unopened from your birthday.

O, there are so many hand-crafted presents
That have been sent to your life
From God.

> —Hafiz, "So Many Gifts"
> *Translated by Daniel Ladinsky*

Extraordinary afflictions are not always the punishment of extraordinary sins, but sometimes the trial
of extraordinary graces—sanctified afflictions are
spiritual promotions.

> —Matthew Henry

For as we venture forth today,
know that you will see
a better day.
For the rumblings of the Earth
will bring forth a dawn
of total goodness in mankind.
And all the suffering and hate and sadness
will be banished from our paradise
and be buried in the womb of Mother Earth
to be our jewels of the future.

Observe the transformation,
know, love, and respect yourself.
For it is in the love that we feel for ourselves
that will dissolve the salts of fear
and the bitterness of hate.

Know who you are, be kind to yourself,
forgive yourself. Effortlessly ride
your swell through life,
gliding through the ups and downs.
Always know there
is a peaceful retreat inside
that no other energy
can invade or destroy.
Hello.

—Deborah Clark

O Mother of Perpetual Help, with greatest confidence I present myself to you. I implore your help
in the problems of my daily life. Have pity on me,
compassionate Mother. Take care of my needs;
free me from my sufferings or if it be the will of
God that I should suffer still longer, grant that I
may endure all with love and patience. Mother of
Perpetual Help I ask this in your love and power.
Amen.

—Catholic prayer

Come tell me of thine ordeal . . .
　　—Homer, seventh century

Every poem is a journey.
Every journey is a meandering stream of words.
Every adventure is a poem awaiting its poet.
What is required of the king within you
Is a valiant effort to hold on to the creaking helm
Of your ship as you plunge forward to get home
　　again,
Shipwrecked, thrown off course, the only one to
　　survive
The temptations of monsters, goddesses, and
　　revenge,
The thought of returning to your voluptuous bride
And fatherless son, who have been waiting for you
Since the red dawn of time, and now are
Ravaged by uncertainty whether it's you
Or a phantom, a shade, or an avenger,
Who's taken your place.

Every title appears when you've reached home,
Which is why we call the deep longing *nostalgia,*
The coming home stories, the return to where it all
　　began.

The real thing is an odyssey.
The real journey is long and lurching, changing
    everything,
The real pilgrimage endures the hell that is that
    change.

Warriors, words, or wizards.
As if there's any difference.
    —Phil Cousineau, "The Real Odyssey"

Dead my old fine hopes
And dry my dreaming but still . . .
Iris, blue each spring
    —Shushiki

Cast thy burden on the Lord;
Only lean upon His word:
Thou shalt soon have cause to bless
His eternal faithfulness.

Ever in the raging storm
Thou shalt see His cheering form,
Hear His pledge of coming aid:
"It is I, be not afraid."

Cast thy burden at His feet;
Linger at His mercy seat:
He will lead thee by the hand
Gently to the better land.

He will gird thee by His power,
In thy weary, fainting hour:
Lean, then, loving, on His word;
Cast thy burden on the Lord.

    —Author unknown

True contentment is a thing as active as agriculture.
It is the power of getting out of any situation all
that there is in it. It is arduous and it is rare. The
absence of this digestive talent is what makes so
cold and incredible the tales of so many people,
who say they have been "through" things; when it
is evident that they have come out on the other
side quite unchanged.

    —G. K. Chesterton

I thank God for my handicaps, for, through them, I
have found myself, my work, and my God.

    —Helen Keller

Oh yes, fix me, Jesus, fix me.
Fix me so that I can walk on
a little while longer.
Fix me so that I can pray on
just a little bit harder.
Fix me so that I can sing on
just a little bit louder.
Fix me so that I can go on despite the pain,
The fear, the doubt, and, yes, the anger.
I ask not that you take this cross from me,
only that you give me the strength to continue
carrying it onward 'til my dying day.
Oh, fix me, Jesus, fix me.

—African American spiritual

The chief pang of most trials is not so much the
actual suffering itself as our own spirit of resistance
to it.

—Jean Nicolas Grou

The house was empty
I was eating cold beans, rice with salsa and an
    avocado
It hadn't been the best of days
There were troubles at work
I had some of my own
And these were overshadowed by those of the world

So, I tuned in the airwaves
In the blink of an eye, she, Goddess of the air,
Was asking, "What are you grateful for? Let me
    know."

I was struck—the very idea—what *was* I thankful for?
Stirred and disturbed
A rising maelstrom of unease
Caught my breath—stilled me
I braced
An upwelling force flowed—heating
My heart strained
My eyes brimmed
Over filled
And those precious jewels poured forth

My silent reply to her was for hope
Hope
Was what I was thankful for this Christmas season

Without cause, pause or reason
A simple joy of the breast
Which soothes and warms
As does a yule log glowing in its hearth
Mantled as it is
Mantled as I am
Hope
With so little reason
In fact with none at all
Is the still peace of which the soul sings
In strains so sweet

Hope
Flying in the face of hard nosed facts
Or the perceptions of the mind's simple eye

And it doesn't matter
If it's only you or I
Who harbor its delicious resource
Because, even if that were so
It would be a treasure all the more worthy
Such a rare gift is heaven's breath
It illuminates the transcendent cause or rule
"Hope, the evidence of things unseen . . .
It is the bird that sings
While dawn is still dark"*

---

*Rabindranath Tagore

And it's what I was thankful for
Even though it seemed of no use
When there was no apparent path
No solution, answer or resolution
When nothing provided surcease of the heart's ache
Hope
Needs no evidence
It is the evidence
Hope needs no cause
It is cause enough
Hope can provide where nothing else will
For it needs nothing, is nothing
Takes nothing
While giving it all away
It's as timely as your next wish
No farther away than your next breath
As intimate as each and every heartbeat must be

Hope, dear friends
Hope is what I was thankful for
That's what I would have told her
If I could have gotten through on that lone and low
    wintry day.
     —Daniel Brady, "Hope"

He said not: thou shalt not be tempted; thou shalt not be travailed; thou shalt not be afflicted. But He said: thou shalt not be overcome.

God willeth that we take heed of these words and that we be ever strong in such test, in weal and woe. For He loveth and enjoyeth us, and so willeth He that we love and enjoy Him and mightily trust in Him, and all shall be well.

—Julian of Norwich

In order to meet the challenges of time and life, whether it be our personal life, professional life, or global life, we will all have to come into our full medicine.

—Angeles Arrien

I returned to God
What God had given me.

He gave it back again.
Only this time, He said,
"This is not your work.
This is my work I give to you.
Do it for my glory."

"But I don't know how," I said.
"I've tried.
I do not know how
And I cannot bear
To try and try
And get nowhere.
It breaks my heart.
It breaks my heart in two.
As if a child had died.
No, worse!
As if my child had died."

But He said, "Try, try again."

I cried.
I was so terrified.

But He said, "Try again."
So we stood,
Stuck,
Him and me.

Me, hands full of his gifts,
Complaining,
"But, my hands are full!"

And Him saying,
"Do not use your hands."

Then me, protesting,
"But how can I write without my hands?"

And Him, getting really pissed off,
Saying, "You were never
Supposed to use your hands.
You were supposed to use mine."
—Ann Kyle-Brown, "The Gift"

Protect me, O Lord;
My boat is so small,
And your sea is so big.
—Old Breton fishermen's prayer

Have you ever just gazed and appreciated a massive
   redwood tree?
It may well be hundreds of years old.
Appreciate the endless bark and the massive trunk
with roots spreading throughout the ground.
Look up to the sky with amazement to see the very
   top of the redwood
swaying with the wind.
Approach the tree and wrap your arms around the
   trunk
holding tightly.

Listen. Feel. Breathe deeply with intention.
The top of the tree is waving and swaying and yet
the trunk of the tree is steadfast in the earth.
Grounded.
The elements are mingling with the top of this
    ancestor, and yet
this redwood remains grounded.
Undisturbed.
Unaffected by the forces that exist on their own.

At a time in my life when I faced tremendous tur-
    moil I was asked,
"Why are the others standing still creating the con-
    fusion and turmoil,
and yet you are running around the tree?"
Stop running. Ground yourself.
Listen. Feel. Breathe deeply with intention.
    —Vadette Goulet

The afternoon knows what the morning never
suspected.
    —Swedish proverb

Lord have mercy upon me and my soul and my
    spirit
as it is just a soul that searches for your truth and
    wisdom.
Lord I am grateful for the knowledge that leads me
    to you.
Lord forgive the times that I distrust you
and cleanse me from my weaknesses
yet make me understand that it is my weaknesses
which bring me closer to you.
Make me strong . . . make me better . . .
make me a channel of your perfect peace
that I may uphold Your vision for me
'cos God u and I . . . we are *one.*
And I am grateful for that.

There are times when I am so afraid
as I am troubled by my thoughts . . .
I wonder where these thoughts come from.
Take away my fear Lord and help me to see
that I need not be afraid of anything.
As long as there is you, there is me and *we* are
    together.
Help me to see this and help me to realize
that *nothing* can separate me from you . . .
not as long as I believe that you and I are one.

Thank you God for this roller coaster life
and thank you for the times I am on top
and the times I am down
and the times it feels like I am going to have a heart
	attack
from the sheer exhilaration of it all.
Thank you God for abiding with me thro'out
and never letting go of my hand.
For that I am grateful and I thank you!
Amen.

—Desiree Sangeetha

Not only action but also suffering is a way to freedom. In suffering, the deliverance consists in our being allowed to put the matter out of our own hands into God's hands.

—Dietrich Bonhoeffer

Be not perplexed,
Be not afraid,
Everything passes,
God does not change.

Patience wins all things.
He who has God lacks nothing;
God alone suffices.

   —Saint Teresa of Avila

There is nothing—no thing, no person, no experience, no thought, no joy or pain—that cannot be
harvested and used for nourishment on our journey
to God.

   —Macrina Wiederkehr

There is nothing to be gained
   by anticipating misery.
I will find the peace I search for
   if I look within me.

Ultimately the choice is simple:
   I can quit, or
   I can move forward.

   —Judith Garrett Garrison and Scott Sheperd

A great grief has taught me more than any minister,
and when feeling most alone I find refuge in the
Almighty Friend.
—Louisa May Alcott

Promise Yourself
To be so strong that nothing can disturb your peace
of mind.
To talk health, happiness and prosperity to every
person you meet.
To make all your friends feel that there is something
in them.
To look at the sunny side of everything and make
your optimism come true.
To think only of the best, to work only for the best,
and expect only the best.
To be just as enthusiastic about the success of others
as you are about your own.
To forget the mistakes of the past and press on to
the greater achievements of the future.
To wear a cheerful countenance at all times and give
every living creature you meet a smile.
To give so much time to the improvement of your
self that you have no time to criticize others.

To be too large for worry, too noble for anger, too
   strong for fear, and too happy to permit the
   presence of trouble.
   —Author unknown

Reflect upon your present blessings of which every
man has many, not on your past misfortunes of
which all men have some.
   —Charles Dickens

In the margins of his print of a Rembrandt etching
Van Gogh scribbled in truffle black ink,
In media noctic vim suam lex exerit.
"In the middle of the night light spreads its power."
He wrote to his brother Theo
that meditating on the print gave
him the courage to live on broth and coffee
and work all night by gaslight,
the heart to make the darkness tangible,
the spirit to create a cavalcade
of color the world had never seen before.

The old master taught him how
to harness infinity, as if God were starting
the universe all over with a clean palette.

But the painter who moved him most
was the blue-souled, angel-winged Giotto,
who was always full of kindness and enthusiasm
and painted despite being always in pain.

What I would I give to have that faith
That living and working in the margins
Will heal even your fiercest wounds.

—Phil Cousineau, "Marginalia"

To Allah we belong and to him we shall return.
Oh Allah, help me in my calamity and replace it
with good.

—Muslim prayer

Botanists say that trees need the powerful March
winds to flex their trunks and main branches, so
that the sap is drawn up to nourish the budding
leaves. Perhaps we need the gales of life in the same
way, though we dislike enduring them. A blustery
period in our fortunes is often the prelude to a new
spring of life and health, success and happiness,
when we keep steadfast in faith and look to the
good in spite of appearances.

—Jane Truax

When the days are short and hurried
And the evenings long and lonely,
And all the deeds of sunlight
Are seen through glass only,
And I hunger for the solace of water and green,
But the deeds of sunlight only are through glass
	seen.
And I thirst for the air of the oceans and the
	mountains,
But drink the despair of the city's concrete
	fountains,
And all my desires are captured dreams,
And I the dreamer afloat on a stream
That whirls and whirls in a downward spire
While the sun and the moon recede higher and
	higher,
And there is not a single rock to catch ahold,
And there is not a single branch to catch a soul,
And the morning is the evening is tomorrow is
	today,
And sleep but a loss of light to lay
The mind and the body in somnolent gray . . .

Then I take up my pen
And I hold it like an arrow

And I arch back my bow
And aim it at the Sparrow . . .

"Her sweet little breast as vulnerable as I!"

And I shoot her in the heart
Just to hear her cry,
And she sings and she sings and she sings for me,
And her wings span all of eternity,
And she swoops and she soars and she fills the sky
With the flight of the spirit that will not die,
And she sings she is the Sparrow and she is me,
Yes she sings I am the Sparrow
And I am free.
When the days are short and hurried
And the evenings long and lonely,
And all the deeds of sunlight
Are seen through glass only,
Then I take up my pen
And I hold it like an arrow
And I arch back my bow
And fly with the Sparrow.

—Ann Kyle-Brown, "The Sparrow"

The gem cannot be polished without friction, nor man perfected without trials.

—Confucious

God of our life,
there are days when the burdens we carry
chafe our shoulders and weigh us down;
when the road seems dreary and endless,
the skies gray and threatening;
when our lives have no music in them,
and our hearts are lonely,
and our souls have lost their courage.
Flood the path with light,
run our eyes to where
the skies are full of promise;
tune our hearts to brave music;
give us the sense of comradeship
with heroes and saints of every age;
and so quicken our spirits
that we may be able to encourage
the souls of all who journey with us
on the road of life, to your honor and glory.

—Saint Augustine

Lord of the loving heart,
May mine be loving too.
Lord of the gentle hands,
May mine be gentle too.
Lord of the willing feet,
May mine be willing too.
So may I grow more like Thee
In all I say and do.

 —Author unknown

Where do you get the strength to go on, when you
have used up all of your own strength? Where do
you turn for patience when you have run out of
patience, when you have been more patient for more
years than anyone should be asked to be, and the
end is nowhere in sight? I believe that God gives us
strength and patience and hope, renewing our spiritual resources when they run dry.

 —Harold Kushner

I am here abroad,
I am here in need,
I am here in pain,

I am here in straits,
I am here alone.
O God, aid me.
     —Celtic prayer

Whatever happens, abide steadfast in a determina-
tion to cling simply to God.
     —Francis de Sales

Ashes my burnt hut . . .
But wonderful the cherry
Blooming on my hill
     —Hokushi

Become a possibilitarian. No matter how dark
things seem to be or actually are, raise your sights
and see possibilities—always see them, for they're
always there.
     —Norman Vincent Peale

O Thou, the Captain of my salvation, strengthen me inwardly and outwardly that I may be vigorous with spiritual purpose and disposed to every virtuous and gallant undertaking. Grant that I may do valiantly despite slothfulness or timidity, and that neither my fear of ridicule nor my love of popularity may make me seem to like what is not right. Be Thou pleased also to fortify my spirit so that I may meet life hopefully and be able to endure everything which Thou mayest be pleased to send me.

—Author unknown

We could never learn to be brave or patient if there were only joy in the world.

—Helen Keller

If we are to continue our evolutionary journey, it is imperative that we now make some equally prodigious leaps in our ability to transform our minds. We must wake up and develop the wisdom that will allow us to use our new powers for our own good and for the good of all. This is the challenge of our times.

—Peter Russell

The suffering that comes to us has a purpose. . . .
It is trying to teach us something. We should look
for its lesson. . . .

    —Peace Pilgrim

In our end is our beginning; in our time, infinity;
In our doubt there is believing, in our life, eternity,
In our death, a resurrection; at the last, a victory,
Unrevealed until its season, something God alone
can see.

    —Methodist hymn

It is only a tiny rosebud,
A flower of God's design;
But I cannot unfold the petals
With these clumsy hands of mine.
The secret of unfolding flowers
Is not known to such as I.
God opens this flower so sweetly,
Then in my hand they die.
If I cannot unfold a rosebud,
This flower of God's design,

Then how can I have the wisdom
To unfold this life of mine?
So I'll trust in Him for leading
Each moment of my day.
I will look to Him for His guidance
Each step of the pilgrim way.
The pathway that lies before me,
Only my Heavenly Father knows.
I'll trust Him to unfold the moments,
Just as He unfolds the rose.

    —Author unknown

Sometimes our fate resembles a fruit tree in winter.
Who would think that those branches would turn
green again and blossom, but we hope it, we know it.

    —Johann Wolfgang von Goethe

Your circumstances may be uncongenial, but they
shall not long remain so if you but perceive an ideal
and strive to reach it. You cannot travel *within* and
stand still *without*. . . .

    Whatever your present environment may be,
you will fall, remain, or rise with your thoughts,
your vision, your ideal. You will become as small as

your controlling desire; as great as your dominant aspiration.

—James Allen

The universe is transformation—our life is what our thoughts make it.

—Marcus Aurelius

God, make me brave for life:
oh, braver than this.
Let me straighten after pain,
as a tree straightens after the rain,
Shining and lovely again.

God, make me brave for life;
much braver than this.
As the blown grass lifts,
let me rise
From sorrow with quiet eyes,
knowing Thy way is wise.

God, make me brave, life brings
such blinding things.
Help me to keep my sight;

help me to see aright
that out of dark comes light.
　　—Author unknown

Keep your face in the sunshine and the shadows will
fall behind you.
　　—Irish proverb

O Cosmic Birther of all radiance and vibration!
　　Soften the ground of our being
and carve out a space within us where your presence
　　can abide.
Fill us with your creativity so that we may be
　　empowered to bear
the fruit of your mission.
Let each of our actions bear fruit in accordance
　　with our desire.
Endow us with the wisdom to produce and share
　　what each being needs
to grow and flourish. Untie the tangled threads of
　　destiny that bind us,
as we release others from the entanglement of past
　　mistakes.

Do not let us be seduced by that which would
    divert us from our true purpose,
but illuminate the opportunities of the present
    moment.
For you are the ground and fruitful vision, the
    birth, power and fulfillment,
as all is gathered and made whole once again.

—Diarmuid O'Murchu, "The Lord's Prayer"

Gray skies are just clouds passing over.

—Duke Ellington

Dear God, guide me to always have trust in you.
When I am confused or distressed, or feeling fear or
    pain,
Remind me of your loving presence.
Assist me to look beyond appearances and see the
    Truth.

—Author unknown

Have courage for the great sorrows of life and patience for the small ones; and when you have laboriously accomplished your daily task, go to sleep in peace. God is awake.

   —Victor Hugo

As the rain hides the stars, as the autumn mist hides the hills, as the clouds veil the blue of the sky, so the dark happenings of my lot hide the shining of your face from me. Yet, if I may hold your hand in the darkness, it is enough. Since I know that, though I may stumble in my going, you do not fall.

   —Celtic prayer

You will not grow if you sit in a beautiful flower garden, but you will grow if you are sick, if you are in pain, if you experience losses, and if you do not put your head in the sand, but take the pain and learn to accept it, not as a curse or punishment but as a gift to you with a very, very specific purpose.

   —Elisabeth Kübler-Ross

Not given but made,
Not bought but cut.
Not polished, but engraved
With a tool, a *kharaker*,
Sharp enough to cut stone,
Incisive enough to carve away
Unnecessary material,
Reveal essential grain,
Forge deep grooves,
Unleash soul forces
In the lived-in face,

Character, that is.

Your fate, if handed
To you, destiny if
Taken into your
Own hands.

Not built,
Revealed.

If every word was once a poem,
So was every face.

No one wants to admit how deep the cuts are.
Life has a way of being what it is.
　　　—Phil Cousineau, "Building Character"

Those who have suffered much are like those who know many languages; they have learned to understand and to be understood by all.

—Madame Swetchine

O God, help me to think of Thee in this bitter trial. Thou knowest how my heart is rent with grief. In my weakness, tested so severely in soul by this visitation, I cry unto Thee, Father of all life: give me fortitude to say with Thy servant Job: "The Lord hath given; the Lord hath taken away; blessed be the name of the Lord."

Forgive the thoughts of my rebellious soul. Pardon me in these first hours of my grief, if I question Thy wisdom and exercise myself in things too high for me. Grant me strength to rise above this trial, to bear with humility life's sorrows and disappointments. Be nigh unto me, O God. Bring consolation and peace to my soul.

Praised art Thou, O God, who comfortest the mourners. Amen.

—Author unknown

The most important lesson that man can learn from his life is not that there is pain in this world, but that it depends upon him to turn it into good account, that it is possible for him to transmute it into joy.

—Rabindranath Tagore

Do not look forward to the changes and chances of this life in fear; rather look to them with full hope that, as they arise, God, whose you are, will deliver you out of them. He has kept you hitherto—do you but hold fast to His dear hand, and He will lead you safely through all things; and, when you cannot stand, He will bear you in His arms. Do not look forward to what may happen tomorrow; the same everlasting Father who cares for you today will take care of you tomorrow, and every day. Either He will shield you from suffering, or He will give you unfailing strength to bear it. Be at peace, then, and put aside all anxious thoughts and imaginations.

—Francis de Sales

That the birds of worry fly above your head,
This you cannot control.

But that they build nests in your hair,
This you can prevent.
   —Chinese proverb

You must understand the whole of life, not just one
little part of it. That is why you must read, that is
why you must look at the skies, that is why you
must sing, and dance, and write poems, and suffer,
and understand, for all that is life.
   —J. Krishnamurti

In that moment you are drunk on yourself,
The friend seems a thorn,
In that moment you leap free of yourself,
    what use is the friend?
In that moment you are drunk on yourself,
You are the prey of a mosquito,
And the moment you leap free of yourself,
    you go elephant hunting.
In that moment you are drunk on yourself,
You lock yourself away in cloud after
    cloud of grief,
And in that moment you leap
    free of yourself,

The moon catches you and hugs you
    in its arms.
That moment you are drunk on yourself,
    the friend abandons you.
That moment you leap free of yourself,
    the wine of the friend,
In all its brilliance and dazzle,
    is held out to you.
That moment you are drunk on yourself,
You are withered, withered like
    autumn leaves.
That moment you leap free of yourself,
Winter to you appears in the dazzling
    robes of spring.
All disquiet springs from the
    search for quiet.
Look for disquiet and you will come
    suddenly on a field of quiet.
All illnesses spring from the
    scavenging for delicacies.
Renounce delicacies and poison itself will
    seem delicious to you.
All disappointments spring from your
    hunting for satisfactions.
If only you could stop, all imaginable joys
Would be rolled like pearls to your feet.

Be passionate for the friend's tyranny,
    not his tenderness,
So the arrogant beauty in you can become
    a lover that weeps. . . .
    —From a poem by Rumi
        Translated by Andrew Harvey

I would rather walk with God in the dark than go
alone in the light.
    —Mary Gardiner Brainard

The wonder is that, as we walk it, the path becomes
clear. We have only to trust it into action, then
truth reveals itself, shining all the brighter for the
darkness of our time.
    —Joanna Macy

No need for fear
Or deep despair
Seekers of God
Receive his care.

No need for fear
Or deep despair
We are at home
And God is there.
  —Saint Teresa of Avila

It is a basic principle of spiritual life that we learn
the deepest things in unknown territory. Often it is
when we feel most confused inwardly and are in the
midst of our greatest difficulties that something new
will open.

We awaken most easily to the mystery of life
through our weakest side. The areas of our greatest
strength, where we are the most competent and
clearest, tend to keep us away from the mystery.
  —Jack Kornfield

Suffering turns the mind towards God. Suffering
infuses mercy in the heart and softens it. Suffering
strengthens. . . .
  —Sivananda

Beloved Friend God, a few weeks ago everything seemed so clear. I was positive I knew where I was going and what was coming into my life. So many things happened that seemed to support that awareness.

But now, Beloved, it appears that obstacles have been placed in the way of the good I desire. "Little Me" wants to strike out, to demand my good, to manipulate, as I feel things are being manipulated against me.

Yet, Beloved, I know in my Soul that this is another opportunity to surrender to Your Infinite Wisdom and learn the lesson this experience brings, another opportunity to trust You who have led me through many dark nights to greater good.

So, Beloved, aware of your guiding Presence, I take a step in the fog of uncertainty and trust. I take another step and trust. Step by step I move forward, trusting that the fog will pass away before the radiant Light of spiritual understanding and You will bring me to the place You have prepared for me.

I allow You to have Your perfect way with me. I surrender to the highest and best for all concerned. Thank you, Beloved Friend God.

—Kathryn Brenson

We shall steer safely through every storm, so long as our heart is right, our intention fervent, our courage steadfast, and our trust fixed on God. If at times we are somewhat stunned by the tempest, never fear. Let us take breath, and go on afresh.

    —Francis de Sales

Peace does not mean to be in a place where there is no noise, trouble or hard work. It means to be in the midst of those things and still remain calm in your heart.

    —Author unknown

To be afraid of change is to doubt the providence of God. It is an unintelligent fear of the unknown. If it were not for the blessings of change, man would still be primitive savages living in caves, and you yourself would still be a child mentally and physically, would you not? Welcome any change that comes into any phase of your life; insist that it is going to turn out for the better—and it will. See the Angel of God in it, and the Angel of God will make all things new.

—Emmet Fox

There is an alchemy in sorrow. It can be transmuted into wisdom, which, if it does not bring joy, can yet bring happiness.

—Pearl S. Buck

Where faith is there is courage, there is fortitude, there is steadfastness and strength. . . . Faith bestows that sublime courage that rises superior to the troubles and disappointments of life, that acknowledges no defeat except as a step to victory; that is strong to endure, patient to wait, and energetic to struggle. . . . Light up, then, the lamp of faith in your heart. . . . It will lead you safely through the mists of doubt and the black darkness of despair; along the narrow, thorny ways of sickness and sorrow, and over the treacherous places of temptation and uncertainty.

—James Allen

Give thanks for unknown blessings already on their way.

—Native American saying

I hope to be remembered . . .
As someone who lived on Earth
Expressed compassion to creation
Listened deeply with my heart
And experienced communion
With those most neglected and abused.
As someone whose acts of creativity
Lived on after my time,
Projects and people enveloped in the beauty of
    creation
Communing with the recesses of my soul.
As someone who embraced fully
The beauty and brokenness of life
The hopes, joys and sorrows of the moment
And worked to make them gestures of generosity
To heal a brokenhearted world.
And to say when it is finished
    I am grateful
    I have done my best
    I have no regrets
    —James Conlon, "I Hope to Be Remembered"

Prayers for Our Relationships

Love wants to reach out and manhandle us,
Break all our teacup talk of God.

If you had courage and
Could give the Beloved His choice, some nights,
He would just drag you around the room
By your hair,
Ripping from your grip all those toys in the world
That bring you no joy.

Love sometimes gets tired of speaking sweetly
And wants to rip to shreds
All your erroneous notions of truth

That make you fight within yourself, dear one,
And with others,

Causing the world to weep
On too many fine days.

God wants to manhandle us,
Lock us inside of a tiny room with Himself
And practice His dropkick.

The Beloved sometimes wants
To do us a great favor:

Hold us upside down
And shake all the nonsense out.

But when we hear
He is in such a "playful drunken mood"

Most everyone I know
Quickly packs their bags and hightails it
Out of town.

> —Hafiz, "Tired of Speaking Sweetly"
> *Translated by Daniel Ladinsky*

Darkness cannot drive out darkness; only light can
do that. Hate cannot drive out hate; only love can
do that.

> —Martin Luther King Jr.

May we live in peace without weeping.
May our joy outline the lives we touch without
    ceasing.
And may our love fill the world, angel wings
    tenderly beating.
   —Irish prayer

FOR RHINO

The venerable old word comes down
To us from the Norse, like the prow
Of a ship splitting the fog.

Angr, its bog-rich roots suggest,
Means far more than fury,
Rage, ire, or wrath,

Instead, the sagas say, anger reflects
Profoundly felt grief about what's
Gone wrong with the world.

Not blue-nosed, bad-tempered, knee-jerk
Reactions to life's inevitable misfortunes,
But red-faced insight into its avoidable injustices.

Anger, for instance, about the loss of an uncommon
  man,
One who gave a voice to some, wings to others,
  medicine to many.
A man I like to believe was thinking about something miraculous,

Let's say the heart-swelling news from his won-
  drously happy daughter
That he was finally going to be a grandfather,

As his plane banked, sputtered,
And fell from the sky.

If you're never angry, sang the Viking skalds
In the great mead halls after battle,
You're still unborn.
      —Phil Cousineau, "The True Origins of Anger"

Never does a man know the force that is in him
until some mighty affection or grief has humanized
the soul.
      —F. W. Robertson

In everyone there is something precious, found in no one else; so honor each man for what is hidden within him—for what he alone has, and none of his fellows.

—Hasidic saying

When your voice is irritating and I do not have the
    patience to listen
See the Divine Mystery deep inside
When you are old and withered and wrinkled
See the Divine Mystery deep inside
When you take my parking space that I've been
    waiting for
See the Divine Mystery deep inside
When you are the gun-crazed maniac shooting up
    the mall
See the Divine Mystery deep inside
When you are the homeless, dirty, disheveled per-
    son on the street
See the Divine Mystery deep inside
When you are righteous, racist, sexist
See the Divine Mystery deep inside
When you have left your body and only your spirit
    remains
See the Divine Mystery deep inside
When you are drug-crazed
See the Divine Mystery deep inside

When you have left your mind and do not know
    my name
See the Divine Mystery deep inside
When I am the crabgrass or the weed
See the Divine Mystery deep inside
    —Judith McWalter-Sante, "Litany of the
      Crabgrass and the Weeds"

Perceive all conflict as patterns of energy seeking
harmonious balance as elements in a whole.
    —Dhyani Ywahoo

For me holiness is a not a state or a condition, like
a special badge or suit of clothes I may wear. It's
not like a graduate degree or certificate that I earn
through study. It's not even an "energy" or a charis-
matic presence. . . . Holiness instead emerges from
relationship. It's dynamic. It's a manifestation of
what is happening between me and another in the
moment. Was Mother Teresa a holy person treating
the poor and the ill in Calcutta, or was she a person
who was holy while treating the poor and the ill in
Calcutta?
    —David Spangler

Love doesn't just sit there like a stone, it has to be made, like brick; re-made all the time, made new.

   —Ursula K. LeGuin

The most lovable quality any human being can
   possess is tolerance. . . .
It is the vision that enables one to see things from
   another's viewpoint. . . .
It is the generosity that concedes to others the right
   to their own opinions
   and their own peculiarities. . . .
It is the bigness that enables us to let people be
   happy in their own way
   instead of our way.

   —Author unknown

Whenever you see a fault in others, attribute it to yourself. That way you will get the benefit and will learn from others' mistakes.

   —Old Kadampa saying

I've learned
that you cannot make someone love you.
All you can do is be someone who can be
loved. The rest is up to them.

I've learned
that no matter how much I care,
some people just don't care back.

I've learned
that it takes years to build up trust,
and only seconds to destroy it.

I've learned
that it's not what you have in your life
but who you have in your life that counts.

I've learned
that you can get by on charm for about
fifteen minutes.
After that, you'd better know something.

I've learned
that you shouldn't compare
yourself to the best others can do.

I've learned
that you can do something in an instant
that will give you heartache for life.

I've learned
that it's taking me a long time
to become the person I want to be.

I've learned
that you should always leave loved ones
with loving words. It may be the last
time you see them.

I've learned
that you can keep going
long after you can't.

I've learned
that we are responsible for what we do,
no matter how we feel.

I've learned
that either you control your attitude
or it controls you.

I've learned
that regardless of how hot and steamy
a relationship is at first, the passion fades
and there had better be something else to
take its place.

I've learned
that heroes are the people
who do what has to be done
when it needs to be done,
regardless of the consequences.

I've learned
that money is a lousy way of keeping score.

I've learned
that my best friend and I can do anything
or nothing and have the best time.

I've learned
that sometimes the people you expect
to kick you when you're down
will be the ones to help you get back up.

I've learned
that sometimes when I'm angry
I have the right to be angry,
but that doesn't give me
the right to be cruel.

I've learned
that true friendship continues to grow,
even over the longest distance.
Same goes for true love.

I've learned
that just because someone doesn't love
you the way you want them to doesn't
mean they don't love you with all they have.

I've learned
that maturity has more to do with
what types of experiences you've had
and what you've learned from them
and less to do with how many
birthdays you've celebrated.

I've learned
that your family won't always be there for you.
It may seem funny, but people you aren't
related to can take care of you and love you
and teach you to trust people again. Families
aren't biological.

I've learned
that no matter how good a friend is,
they're going to hurt you every once in a while
and you must forgive them for that.

I've learned
that it isn't always enough to be forgiven by
others. Sometimes you are to learn to forgive
yourself.

I've learned
that no matter how bad your heart is broken
the world doesn't stop for your grief.

I've learned
that our background and circumstances
may have influenced who we are,
but we are responsible for who we become.

I've learned
that just because two people argue,
it doesn't mean they don't love each other
and just because they don't argue,
it doesn't mean they do.

I've learned
that we don't have to change friends
if we understand that friends change.

I've learned
that you shouldn't be so eager to find out a
secret. It could change your life forever.

I've learned
that two people can look at the exact same thing
and see something totally different.

I've learned
that no matter how you try to protect your
children, they will eventually get hurt and
you will hurt in the process.

I've learned
that your life can be changed in a matter of
hours by people who don't even know you.

I've learned
that even when you think you have no more
to give, when a friend cries out to you,
you will find the strength to help.

I've learned
that credentials on the wall
do not make you a decent human being.

I've learned
that the people you care about most in life
are taken from you too soon.

—Author unknown (Internet chain letter, 1999)

Though time and distance has placed us in separate
    worlds,
The universal feelings of loss and grief, concern and
    compassion,

Place us in one reality.
May you one day find peace and joy in your
memories.

   —Pamela Ayo Yetunde

May I be no man's enemy, and may I be the friend
of that which is eternal and abides.
May I never quarrel with those nearest to me: and if
I do, may I be reconciled quickly.
May I love, seek, and attain only that which is good.
May I wish for all men's happiness and envy none.
May I never rejoice in the ill fortune of one who
has wronged me.
May I win no victory that harms either me or my
opponent.

   —Eusebius

Loving, like prayer, is a power as well as a process.
It's curative. It is creative.

   —Zona Gale

Creative force, creating still,
Thank you for my beloved [cat's/dog's name].

In a world of uncertainty, her love was constant.
She entertained me and kept me company.
Her brief little life was a gift that
Enriched and deepened my own.
But pets are companions only
For a portion of our journeys.
And now she is gone,
Leaving
A hole in my heart,
An empty spot on my shoulder
And a silence in my ear.
I have known her always by
Her sweet devoted presence and sly playfulness.
From now on, I will love her in her absence.
There may be other cats to keep me company in life.
There will never be another [cat's name].
For [cat's name], O Gracious Wisdom,
I am truly grateful.

Alternative stanza for losing a dog:
 . . . And now he is gone,
Leaving a hole in my heart,
An empty spot on my couch.
No wagging tail greets me
And no one wriggles with delight as I return home.
I have known him always by . . .

   —Ann Keeler Evans, "Prayer on Losing Your
     Cat [Dog]"

Silence exists in me.
There are no words for the
    loss I feel.
The only sound I hear is
    the song of your caring.
    —Judith Garrett Garrison and Scott Sheperd

Fly on, dear ones, fly on
    children of our nest,
    babes of my breast,
Fly on.

Fly on into the infinite reaches of your souls,
    Into the vast potential of your unfolding
        futures,
Fly on dear ones, fly on.

Dig for juicy worms in the rich earth,
    Seek out the updrafts
        Soar within the heavens.
Fly on dear ones, fly on.

Your father and I, our home, our love
are merely the foundation,

the springboard, the nest
from which to fly from.
As you fly, so do we.
    Stretched out and multiplied
    into the future with no controls.
Just the loving expression of a larger Source
    giving birth to life and
    blessing the process of discovery,
    the rich choices of expression,
    and the humility that we too must die.

Take flight my children,
    And carry with you
        our blessing on your becoming, and
        our love that can never die.
For it is not of our creation,
    it is the grace and beauty of creation itself.

Fly on children, fly on.
    —Judy Tretheway

There is so much good in the worst of us,
And so much bad in the best of us,
That it hardly becomes any of us
To talk about the rest of us.
    —Author unknown

Keep me from
judging you
when I feel
that you have
shut me off
and dismissed me.

Keep me from
making you ugly
when I feel
unappreciated and
misunderstood.

Keep me from
closing my heart
against you, and against myself,
because I wanted to connect
with you
and didn't.

Keep me from
wanting to punish you
because we weren't connecting
at a certain moment
in time.

Keep me from
repeating this pattern
and making myself,
and you, wrong, again and again.
It was just a moment.
It is not this moment.
—Margaret Jain

To let go is not to adjust everything to my own
    desires—
But to take each day as it comes and cherish myself
    in it.

To let go is not to judge—
But to allow another to be a human being.

To let go is not to try to change or blame another—
It is to make the most of myself.

To let go is not to regret the past—
But to grow and live for the future.

To let go is to fear less—and to love more.
    —Author unknown

Life is short and we have not too much time for
gladdening the hearts of those who are traveling the
dark way with us. Oh, be swift to love! Make haste
to be kind!
  —Henri F. Amiel

Why, sir, do you get angry at someone
Who is angry with you?
What are you going to gain by it?
How is he going to lose by it?
Your physical anger brings dishonor on yourself:
Your mental anger disturbs your thinking.
How can the fire in your house burn the neighbor's
    house
Without engulfing your own?
  —Basavanna

Lord of the World, I stand before you and before
my neighbors—pardoning, forgiving, struggling
to be open to all who have hurt and angered me.
Be this hurt of body or soul, of honor or property,

whether they were forced to hurt me or did so will-
ingly, whether by accident or intent, whether by
word or deed—I forgive them because we are
human. . . . I am ready to take upon myself the
commandment, Love your neighbor as yourself.

—Levi Yitchak of Beditschev

Blessed are they who understand
my faltering steps and palsied hand.

Blessed are they who know my ears today
must strain to catch the things they say.

Blessed are they who seem to know
that my eyes are dim and wits are slow.

Blessed are they who looked away
when coffee spilled at the table today.

Blessed are they who never say,
"You've told that story twice today."

Blessed are they who know the way
to bring back memories of yesterday.

Blessed are they who know I'm at a loss
to find the strength to carry the cross.

Blessed are they who ease the days
on my journey home in loving ways.
    —Author unknown

The love of our neighbor in all its fullness simply
means being able to say, "What are you going
through?"
    —Simone Weil

Lord, remember all who are single and lonely.
Lord, remember all who cannot sleep,
Do not want to sleep or sleep fitfully.
Lord, remember all people in relationships—
The sacrifices, the getting on together,
The space or lack of it.
Lord, remember all who feel downtrodden,
Victimized or unfairly treated.
Lord, remember all who find no point,
Value or meaning in living.

Finally Lord, remember any who suffer,
No matter what form the suffering takes,
And may it bear fruit
Even if this fruit is unknown to the sufferer
Or known only in hindsight.
　　—Author unknown

Easy for all to offer in worship a green leaf to the
Lord. Easy for all to give a mouthful to the cow.
Easy for all to give a handful when sitting down to
eat. Easy for all to speak pleasant words to others.
　　—Tirumantiram

If I have harmed anyone in any way
either knowingly or unknowingly
through my own confusions
I ask their forgiveness.

If anyone has harmed me in any way
either knowingly or unknowingly
through their own confusions
I forgive them
And if there is a situation
I am not yet ready to forgive
I forgive myself for that.

For all the ways that I harm myself,
negate, doubt, belittle myself,
judge or be unkind to myself
through my own confusions
I forgive myself.

    —Buddhist prayer

We spend all of our time acquiring things, possessions, and protecting our possessions, and sometimes it takes real tragedies in life to bring us to the
point where we understand what really counts; that
is friends, families, and helping other people.

    —Alan Harris

All that we ought to have
    thought and have not thought,
All that we ought to have said, and
    have not said,
All that we ought to have done, and
    have not done;

All that we ought not to have
    thought, and yet have thought,

All that we ought not to have
    spoken, and yet have spoken,
All that we ought not to have done,
    and yet have done;
For thoughts, words and works,
    pray we, O God, for forgiveness.
    —Persian prayer

What greater thing is there for two human souls
than to feel that they are joined for life—to
strengthen each other in all labor, to rest on each
other in all sorrow, to minister to each other in all
pain . . .
    —George Eliot

Grief knits two hearts in closer bonds than happiness ever can, and common suffering is a far
stronger link than common joy.
    —Alphonse de Lamartine

Love of my life
You hold my heart in yours as
I awaken to the depths and desperation of our love.

How can I share you with God?

I cling to you.
Each breath, each smile, each pulse
is so very precious,
pregnant with its intensity.
Alive for yet another moment.

And yet I know somehow I must let go.
Unwrap my grip on our togetherness
Shift my clinging into an offering

I want you to be only mine
And yet love's greater song calls.
It's time to share you, release you
Open my heart and let you soar . . .

—Judy Tretheway, "Be Mine . . . Not God's:
February 6, 2001"

O Great Spirit, whose care reaches to the uttermost
parts of the earth; we humbly beseech thee to
behold and bless those whom we love, now absent

from us, and defend them from all dangers of soul
and body.

—Adapted from The Book of Common Prayer

Do not stand by my grave and weep.
I am not there. I do not sleep—
I am a thousand winds that blow,
I am the diamond glints on snow,
I am the sunlight on ripened grain,
I am the gentle autumn rain.
Do not stand by my grave and cry.
I am not there. I did not die.

—Author unknown

Think of someone you find difficult to deal with
or forgive. Be aware of your inner experience when
you think of this person. Notice how you feel
inside. Now ask yourself, "Do I like feeling this
way? Do I want to experience freedom from this
constriction, pain, anger, or fear that I am carrying?"

Remind yourself that you deserve happiness and
freedom from suffering, because that is God's Will
for you. You may need to take that on faith right
now, but be willing to do that, just for this moment.

Say in your mind, "I am entitled to healing and release from this fear and pain, because that is God's Will for me. I am willing to receive that healing." And now make a clear choice—inwardly take a stand—for your own freedom, for your own healing. Take a deep breath, and feel the sense of inner strength that comes from aligning your own will with the Will of God for you.

And recognize that this difficult person in your life is, in some sense, offering you the gift of self-healing—the gift of remembering your real inner strength and spiritual magnitude, the gift of re-connecting with your wholeness, your love, your true Self.

Notice any resistance that comes up inside you to recognizing and receiving that gift. Don't judge the resistance or fight it. Simply breathe and make space for it. Any resistance you feel is simply your ego's fear of healing. It is asking for your acceptance and love, so be merciful toward yourself. Be kind and spacious toward these feelings within you.

And now offer up this prayer for healing:

Beloved Holy Spirit, Spirit of wisdom and love within me, I offer You my relationship with _____ for guidance, inspiration, and healing. I give You all my thoughts, all my judgments, all my perceptions of myself and of _____. I give You all the pain from my past, I give You any investment I have in reliving the past, I give You any attachment I have to being right. Release me from everything within my mind that would keep me bound to limitation, suffering, forgetfulness, and fear. I want to be free. I want to experience my wholeness and my innocence. I do not know the way to healing, but I trust that You do, and so I place my hand in Yours and let You lead me. Please direct my thoughts and guide my vision. Help me to see in this brother or sister only what You would have me see. Help me to see in myself only what You would have me see. Show me the way to healing and to peace. Thank You very much. Amen.

—Diane Berke, "A Prayer Process for Healing Relationships"

Where there is forgiveness, there is God Himself.

—Adi Granth

Divine Spirit, please guide us that we may do here
Whatever is most right:
That we may inflict no harm,
That we may receive no harm,
That we may take no credit,
That we may release all results,
And that we may shine only Your light
Into the lives of those we touch . . .
And so it is!

 —Author unknown

There are glimpses of heaven in every act, or
thought, or word that raises us above ourselves.

 —Arthur Stanley

Great Source
Reveal to my consciousness
The highest total awareness
of expressions of your Being
So that your nature of Peace and Love
And the Power that exists therein
Creates abundant fulfillment
From a stable, secure foundation

In this body/mind/heart, this Soul
Your Spirit—forever.
   —Wendy Wolters

If we could read the secret history of our enemies,
we should find in each man's life sorrow and suffering enough to disarm all hostility.
   —Henry Wadsworth Longfellow

I had to seek the Physician
Because of the pain this world
Caused
Me.

I could not believe what happened when I got
   there—
I found my
Teacher.

Before I left, he said,
"Up for a little homework, yet?"
"Okay," I replied.

"Well then, try thanking all the people
who have caused
you pain.

They helped you
Come to
Me."

> —Kabir, "I Had to Seek the Physician"
> *Translated by Daniel Ladinsky*

The rule for us all is perfectly simple. Do not waste time bothering whether you "love" your neighbor; act as if you did. As soon as we do this we find one of the great secrets. When you are behaving as if you loved someone, you will presently come to love him.

> —C. S. Lewis

May the faith that gives us hope,
May the love that shows the way,
May the peace that cheers the heart,
Be yours this day.

> —Author unknown

Today the sky blew up in Kansas City.

When I was there, the sky was so pale,
So pale—as pale as I looked as I felt
As the blood pumping through
What was passing for a heart.
It was winter in Kansas City
The deepest recesses of my soul
Were as frigid as the wind.
I've always hated the Sky in Winter
In Kansas City.

Does the death of a beloved have a half-life?
I am certainly no more than half alive
Since you sat down on the side of a pool
Those weeks ago and didn't get up.
From where I sit I can't imagine
The numbness will ever leave.

Where did you go when you left?
How can it be that I can't find you?
Where does the love that binds our hearts
Go
When one heart is missing?

I looked at the Frank Stella above Ann's head
When she told the world how much I loved you
And what a precious, precious gift you were.

My heart, frozen inside me, couldn't recognize
The dancing flames,
I saw only a painting.

If someone had told me, I might have understood
That other hearts thawed
As metaphor after metaphor
Struck fire into the ice of Midwestern Homophobia
And Repression.
I'm a rational man, if there's fire, there's you.

But I didn't dare touch the anguish.
Oh, sweetest man, how can you be gone?
And how can I rise up and lie down
With the rhythms of the day?
No. I will not think, I will not feel. I will not.

And yet the flames danced.
On Monday, they died back to an ember:
I couldn't make the journey home
To where there was no heart
If those flames were living fire.
I must have banked them deep inside—
Encasing them with ice.

But you and I—we met in Kansas City.
It was here love leapt for the first time
In our breasts

It was here the sparkle in your eye
Lit the conflagration
That would consume my life
For almost 20 years.
So it's scarcely surprising
That a stray spark would
Be caught by the wind
And ignite the sky.

Too cold for dousing.
Too hot for fighting.
Our love rages out of control
Out in the world,
Outside my heart
Because you no longer contain me.

Today the sky blew up in Kansas City.
And I sat in your closet
And wept.

> —Ann Keeler Evans, "For Bob, who will always
> love Tom"

The deepest level of communication is communion.
It is beyond words, it is beyond speech, and it is
beyond concept. Not that we discover a new unity.
We discover an old unity.

> —Thomas Merton

God make me a little bit kinder,
A little more tender and true,
Not needing constant reminder
Of the things that I know I should do.
God make me more easy to live with
Less ready to get hurt and vexed,
More patient and helpful in dealing
With the worried, the sad, the perplexed.
     —Author unknown

Every act of love
is a work of peace
no matter how small.
     —Mother Teresa

When the heart hurts . . . there's no place to go . . .
     where your world . . . will seem right
But don't pull back . . . as a matter of fact . . . get
     real close . . . and hold tight

I'm right here . . . and you're over there . . . but I
     can still . . . feel your embrace

I'm in your arms . . . as you hold each other . . . my
    hand is on your face

So hold on to each other . . . when you can't hold on
Share your tears . . . quiet your fear . . . and hold on
    to each other

You're not alone . . . you're closer to home than you
    think . . . please confide . . .
in someone who loves you . . . in someone you
    love . . . we all have pain inside

So hold on to each other . . .

*I will call on all the angels . . . they will help you
    make it through the night
You will be surrounded by angels . . . they will let you
    know, I'll be all right*

My spirit lives . . . continues to give . . . I can see . . .
    through your eyes
I'll be there . . . with whomever you hold . . . It's
    beyond . . . the question why

I'm right here . . . and you're over there . . . but I
    can still . . . feel your embrace
I'm in your arms . . . as you love each other . . .
    your hand is on my face

*I will call on all the angels . . . to be with you through
    lonely nights
You will be surrounded by angels . . . they will gently
    help you hold the light
hold the light*

. . . Hold on . . . Hold on . . . to each other
  —Karl Anthony, "Hold On to Each Other"
  (*In memory of Jamie, www.jamiesjoy.org*)

"Come child, be not frightened,
I take you only to another life."

Weak she was, pliant, open,
In no way fearful, or defiant,
Limp she was, eyes beseeching
Guidance, frail arms reaching.

And the dark wings, powerful and soft,
Encircled her and carried her aloft.
  —Ann Kyle-Brown, "The Angel of Death"
  (After the painting *The Angel of Death* by
  Evelyn De Morgan)

What keeps us alive, what allows us to endure?
I think it is the hope of loving,
or being loved.

I heard a fable once about the sun going on a
    journey
to find its source, and how the moon wept
without her lover's
warm gaze.

We weep when light does not reach our hearts.
    We wither
like fields if someone close
does not rain their
kindness
upon
us.
    —Meister Eckhart, "The Hope of Loving"
      Translated by Daniel Ladinsky

What do we live for, if it is not to make life less difficult for each other.
    —George Eliot

We who lived in concentration camps can remember the men who walked through the huts comforting others, giving away their last piece of bread. They may have been few in number, but they offer sufficient proof that everything can be taken away from a man but one thing: the last of the human freedoms—to choose one's attitude in any given set of circumstances, to choose one's own way.

—Victor Frankl

Where there is great love there are always miracles.

—Willa Cather

Endurance, cleanliness,
      strength, purity
Will keep our lives straight
Our actions only for a good
      purpose.
Our words will be truth.
Only honesty shall come from
      our interaction
With all things.

—From the Lakota Sioux Sweat Lodge ceremony

Love needs to be proved by action.
— Saint Thérèse of Lisieux

Not too long ago you felt this tiny being deep
    within your belly.
You cradled her into becoming.
Now she lies dying
cradled in your arms,
Let her love saturate your heart,
Feel blessing upon your future.
Allow her to guide your becoming.

Soon the time will come
And you will no longer be able to hug and
    nuzzle her
But her love will remain to comfort you in your
    sorrow,
To protect you from your own confusion,
To guide you through your despair.

Bear witness to this tiny great love
Allow her to plant the seeds of goodness in your
    heart,

The seeds of potential
The gifts of grace to unfold throughout your life
Guided, guarded by the angel of your tiny dying
   baby.

   —Judy Tretheway, "Janetta's Poem"

I expect to pass through life but once. If, therefore, there be any kindness I can show, or any good thing I can do to any fellow being, let me do it now, for I shall not pass this way again.

   —William Penn

Granting that you and I argue. If you get the better of me, and not I of you, are you necessarily right and I wrong? Or if I get the better of you and not you of me, am I necessarily right and you wrong? Or are we both partly right and partly wrong? Or are we both wholly right and wholly wrong? You and I cannot know this, and consequently we all live in darkness.

   —Chuang Tzu

God of infinite love and understanding,
pour out your healing Spirit upon [name] and
    [name],
as they reflect upon the failure of their marriage and
    make a new beginning.
Where there is hurt or bitterness,
grant healing of memories,
and the ability to put behind the things that are past.

Where feelings of despair or worthlessness flood in,
nurture the spirit of hope and confidence,
that by your grace, tomorrow can be better than
    yesterday.

Where each looks within and discovers faults
that have contributed to the destruction of the
    marriage,
and have hurt other people,
grant forgiveness for what is past,
and growth in all that makes for new life.

Bring healing to their children, and help us minister
    your healing to them.

We pray for other family and friends,
for the healing of their hurts, and the acceptance
    of new realities.

All this we ask in the name of the One
who sets us free from slavery to the past, and makes
    all things new. . . .
Amen.

 —From The United Methodist Book of Worship

It is not who is right, but what is right, that is of
importance.

 —Thomas Huxley

Love seeketh not itself to please
Nor for itself hath any care,
But for another gives its ease
And builds a heaven in hell's despair.

 —William Blake

None of you will have real faith until you wish for
your brother what you want for yourself.

 —Mohammad

Today I heard you had decided
That you were no longer willing to chase cures
At the expense of your life,
That you wanted to claim each moment left to you.
And I wept.
Your battle has been so long.
Your body, so ravaged by treatment and disease.
My dear Friend, I will be so glad when your pain
    relents.
I will support however you live the time that is left
    to you,
But it is not easy to let you go, for I have loved you
    with such joy.

Beloved One, take from me whatever you need.
I will come and chat or clean and sort
Or simply sit in silence—holding you or giving you
    space.
This is your journey to take without me.
But I will keep you company while I can.
I am so sorry and sad.

I promise you now,
I will tell all the wild and gentle stories about you.
I will listen in my heart for your sage advice.

I will celebrate the wisdom we gathered together
(and cherish our foolish adventures!).
I will weep with great abandon,
Miss you beyond contemplation,
Love you eternally.
You have been a blessing in my life,
A gift from the One who gives us Life and Love.
Now, in your name and in my own,
I will offer myself as a blessing to the world.
Safe journey, my Friend,
Safe journey home.

—Ann Keeler Evans, "Prayer Upon Hearing That
a Friend Is Relinquishing the Battle"

I
have a cause.
We need those don't we?
Otherwise the darkness and the cold gets in
and everything starts to
ache.

My soul has a purpose, it is
to love;

if I
do not fulfill
my heart's vocation,
I suffer.

> —Saint Thomas Aquinas, "Otherwise, the
> Darkness"
> *Translated by Daniel Ladinsky*

To love God truly, you must first love man, and if
anyone tells you that he loves God but does not
love his fellow men, he is lying.

> —Hasidic saying

It is easy to love those who live far away. It is not
always easy to love those who live right next to us.
It is easier to offer a dish of rice to meet the hunger
of a needy person than to comfort the loneliness
and the anguish of someone in our own home who
does not feel loved.

I want you to go and find the poor in your
homes. Above all, your love has to start there. I
want you to be the good news to those around you.

> —Mother Teresa

The highest form of wisdom is kindness.
    —Berakoth

We drove in darkness,
the amber lights of Sonoma
receding in my rearview mirror,
shadows leaping like thieves
from eucalyptus trees
along the night road.

How do you lead a child
into the darkness and out again?

What can you say to your young son
after he watches you watching soldiers
shoot children on the evening news?
What can you say when he turns your bones blue
by asking you from the backseat of the car,
"Please, Papa, hold my hand.
It's dark all round me."

The dark word had never sounded so ominous.
I reach across the back seat, feeling velveteen
darkness on my fingertips, and clasp his

trembling hand in my best tough-and-
tender grasp, then hear him whisper,
as if to reassure me:
"Just until it gets light again, Papa."
And now driving one-handed, I listen
for the reassuring sound of sleep, remember
the moment I held him for the first time,
all crinkled and crying, blinking and trying
to open his gummed-up eyes,
startled by all that light
after all that darkness.

Hurtling home past long abandoned railroad tracks
and farm land lost to grapevines, I spin
the green-glowing dial of the car radio
and hear Bruce Springsteen wailing
like a lost locomotive about how
he'd "Drive All Night"
just to be with her,
his love,
his life.

And hearing that lonesome moan, I sing along
until I feel my dead father's voice vibrating
in my throat, sing until I hear traces
of my own voice in my son's as he cries,
"Papa, how much longer? How much longer
is it going to be dark?"

Only then did the words spring free,
the lie I told to tell the longer truth,
"Don't worry, buddy, we'll be home soon.
I won't let the darkness hurt you."

—Phil Cousineau, "With Jack, Age Four, in the Car"

From wherever my children have built their shelters,
May their roads come in safety.
May the forests
And the brush
Stretch out their water-filled arms
And shield their hearts.
May their roads come in safety,
May their roads be fulfilled.

—Zuni prayer

Not on Father's Day, Lord
not today
not now.

Just give me
one more day.
Is it too much for a father to ask?
She's my only child.

I'll go to the cemetery and do what a man's gotta do
But please don't take her while I'm gone
Please let me hold her,
one more time.

The casket I choose will cradle her soon enough.
Oh, cradle me Lord.
Hold me
in my sorrow.

So I can cradle her
one more day.

    —Judy Tretheway, "Father's Day"

Watch, O Lord, with those who wake, or watch, or
    weep tonight,
and give your angels charge over those who sleep.
Tend your sick ones, O Lord Christ.
Rest your weary ones.
Bless your dying ones.
Soothe your suffering ones.
Pity your afflicted ones.
Shield your joyous ones.
And for all your love's sake. Amen.

    —Saint Augustine of Hippo

We ourselves feel that what we are doing is just a drop in the ocean. But if that drop was not in the ocean, I think the ocean would be less because of that missing drop. I do not agree with the big way of doing things. To us what matters is an individual. To get to love the person we must come in close contact with him. If we wait till we get the numbers, then we will be lost in the numbers.

—Mother Teresa

If anyone speaks ill of you,
Praise them always.
If anyone injures you,
Serve them nicely.
If anyone persecutes you,
Help them in all possible ways.
You will attain
Immense strength.
You will control
Anger and pride.
You will enjoy
Peace, poise and serenity.
You will become divine.

—Swami Sivananda

In refusing to be put out and annoyed, you are taking God's hand in yours. And once you feel God's hand, or the hand of anyone that loves good, in yours, let pity take the place of irritation, let silence take the place of a hasty answer.

—Edward Wilson

Forgiveness is not an occasional act; it is a permanent attitude.

—Martin Luther King Jr.

Please if you must go, then let me know . . . where
    will I feel your loving arms
Is it too much to want for the touch . . . I have
    been used to all my life
I am afraid, a decision is made . . . but I am less
    than willing
So if you must go, then let me know . . . where will
    I feel your loving arms

Please could you disguise or look through the
    eyes . . . used by a perfect stranger

Then, whether or not, this lesson is taught . . .
    I will be in your loving arms
In all that I do, I'm thinking of you . . . and it will
    bless my life
So please, if you must go, then let me know . . .
    where will I feel your loving arms
if you must go, then let me know . . . where will I
    feel your loving arms

I am afraid a decision is made . . . and I am less
    than willing . . . so
If you must go, then let me know . . . where will I
    feel your loving arms
If you must go, then let me know . . . where will I
    feel your loving arms
If you must go, then let me know . . . where will I
    feel your . . . loving arms
Please let me feel your . . . loving arms
Please let me feel your . . . loving arms
    —Karl Anthony, "Loving Arms"
    (in memory of my mother)

Love sees things perfect in spite of flaws.
    —James Dillet Freeman

Don't look for the flaws as you go through life,
And even when you find them,
It is wise and kind to be somewhat blind
And look for the virtue behind them.

—Author unknown

You raged
And holding your anger
I listened
To its echoing deeply
Into your life and mine.

Fear and pain
Sent swirls of despair and venom
Around the room.

I stood, grounded, breathing
Hoping to provide an anchor,
A haven,
And yet
I knew
How cleansing and peaceful
It could be tomorrow,
If the storm had its way today.

—Judy Tretheway, "Rage"

We come to love not by finding a perfect person,
but by learning to see an imperfect person perfectly.
　—Sam Keen

When he realized there was no hope for rescue
The Russian lieutenant groped his way through
The luciferous dark to his corner desk
Deep in the steel-ribbed bowels of the submarine.
The bones of his hands ached as he removed
Paper and pen from the sliding metal drawer,
And conjured up the way the summer light
Of St. Petersburg played in his fiancé's long blonde
　hair,
How her soft breath blew softly on his cheek,
Her rosebud lips slipped across his mouth like a
　promise.
The iron walls creaked; seawater leaked in
As the officer steadied his stinging fingers,
slowed down his breath so the last of the oxygen
Would last a few minutes longer. Then he began his
　last letter.
He began with the simple truth,
I am writing blindly.

Resolutely, he continued to write even as darkness
Thickened around the blue flare of his last matches,
And his lungs felt the rising pressure, his ears heard
Rivets popping, the walls crackling like tinfoil,
And one by one the engines, dynamos, and pumps
   faling silent.
Still, he continued, one excruciating word at a time.
He wrote until he could breathe no more.
Weeks later the letter was found under his bloated
   hand by a rescue team
Who delivered it to his fiancé, as if from the next
   world.
It is later than you think.

    —Phil Cousineau, "Writing in the Dark"

Every day, think as you wake up, today I am fortu-
nate to be alive, I have a precious human life, I am
not going to waste it. I am going to use all my ener-
gies to develop myself, to expand my heart out to
others; to achieve enlightenment for the benefit of
all beings. I am going to have kind thoughts
towards others, I am not going to get angry or
think badly about others. I am going to benefit others as much as I can.

    —His Holiness the XIVth Dalai Lama

God has no other hands than ours.

— Dorothee Solle

If we can be courageous, one more time than we are fearful; if we can be trusting, one more time than we are anxious; if we can be cooperative, one more time than we are competitive; if we can be forgiving, one more time than we are vindictive; if we can be loving, one more time than we are hateful . . . we will have moved closer to the next breakthrough in our evolution.

— Jonas Salk

Prayers for Our Communities

There's no question that we are about to come into a global dark night; maybe we've been in it for quite some time, and it's just beginning to catch up with us. We're realizing, "My God, we've forgotten community!" We've become so isolated from one another that now it's the time for all of that to come back together again. . . . I don't think we got into the dark night alone, and we won't get out of it alone.

—Joan Borysenko

For the old black woman in the bright red hat
Who took the cell phone call as the tires of our plane
Screeched against the tarmac at JFK, at 8:50 A.M.,
Her shriek waking up two hundred sleeping
    passengers,

Draining the blood out of the faces of the flight
     attendants:
"They've hit the tower . . . they've hit the tower . . ."

For the father talking furtively to his wife
On his mobile so his young daughters wouldn't
Be more frightened than they already were,
As we stood together in the horseshoe drive
In front of the main terminal, gazing down the
     freeway
To the mushroom cloud rising over the Manhattan
     skyline,
The father who wobbled and fell to his knees
     weeping
When we saw the red and gold flare against the
     second Tower.

For the lawyer in the elevator of the Imperial Hotel
Near Shea Stadium who told me with a death-
     riddled voice
That he'd just moved to New York to work for
     Cantor Fitzgerald,
And now he'd lost everyone he knew in the world,
"But, Oh, do you want to have dinner? I better talk
About this or somebody's going to get hurt."

For the fireman with the thousand-yard stare,
Silhouetted in putrid smoke, his yellow jacket caked

With bone-and-plaster ash from the blackened fire,
Oblivious to the rumbling sounds
Coming from the deep inside the smoking ruins.
When asked in front of a cavalcade of microphones
    and cameras,
How could you keep turning around and return
To the smoking hole in the ground?
He says in a voice dripping with disdain
For the heroically-angling question,
"This is what I do."
Then he turns and walks back
Into the smoking hole,
Like a man looking for his own kids.

For the New York City police officer in the Village
    bar
A world past midnight downing shots of tequila,
Tearing up, admitting he couldn't go home yet
To his wife and kids because he couldn't get
The two jumpers out of his head,
A man and woman on fire,
Who landed, he whispers,
With a dull thud
A few feet
    From him.

For the bookstore, where I was scheduled to sign
    copies
Of my new book, at 11 A.M. that death-vomiting
    morning
Now obliterated, forgotten, incinerated, under a
    black and white
Wave of rubble, glass, stone and ink, paper, blood
    and dust,
For everybody, everything, everywhere
Fallen.

For the night's dead silence in the ghostly void
Where the glassy Twin Towers once stood,
The phantoms who went to work and never left,
The human whirlwinds who fell into the hole of a
    story
That will never be filled, and their dust that now
Blows across the universe.

For the dazed European visitor, too, who went
    looking
Around the Washington Square for some
    explanation,
Ending up at the candle ceremony, sneering in
    disgust
At the MISSING photos taped to the chained-link
    fence,

The mourners singing, at me for weeping,
Declaiming with Biblical certainty,
"This is what we get for being religious."

For the anonymous fingers that drew war's
Weary graffiti: "REVENGE," "KILL," "DEATH!"
Into thick drifts of ash fallen on the windshields
Of pulverized fire trucks, police cars, and taxis.

For all who claim there's a simple explanation
For the cruel radiance of vengeful voices
Calling for death in the name of God,
The vigilantes convulsing with ecstasy
Over their execution of justice,
Remember this ancient threnody:
Things are not what they
Seem to be, nor are
They otherwise.

—Phil Cousineau, "Elegy for the Fallen:
September 14, 2001"

May I be medicine for those who are sick, a partner
for those who are lonely, a bridge for those who need
to cross over, and a light for those who are blind.

—Prayer of the Bodhisattva

Do all the good you can
By all the means you can
In all the ways you can
In all the places you can
To all the people you can
As long as ever you can.

　　　—John Wesley

The real quest for today is living our individual authenticity in community, where we're powerful as individuals—and together, as individuals in our authenticity, we are much more.

　　　—Michael Toms

Sympathy sees and says, "I'm sorry."
Compassion sees and says, "I'll help."
When we learn the difference,
we can make a difference.

　　　—Author unknown

While I turned my head
That traveler I'd just passed . . .
Melted into mist
 —Shiki

Source and goal
of community,
whose will it is that all
your people enjoy
fullness of life:
may we be builders
of community,
caring for your
good earth
here and world-wide
and as partners with the poor,
signs of your
ever friendly love;
that we may delight in diversity
and choose solidarity
for you are in
community with us
our God forever.
 —Author unknown

Because of the interconnectedness of all minds,
affirming a positive vision may be about the most
sophisticated action any one of us can take.

—Willis Harman

Wage peace with your breath.
Breathe in firemen and rubble.
Breathe out whole buildings and flocks of red-wing
    blackbirds.
Breathe in terrorists
Breathe out sleeping children and fresh mown
    fields.
Breathe in confusion and breathe out maple trees.
Breathe in the fallen and breathe out lifelong
    relationships intact.

Wage peace with our listening: hearing sirens, pray
    loud.
Remember your tools: flower seeds, clothing pins,
    clean rivers.
Make soup.
Play music; learn the word "thank you" in 3
    languages.

Learn to knit: make a hat.
Think of chaos as dancing raspberries.
Imagine grief at the outbreak of beauty or gesture
    of fish.
Swim for the other side.

Wage peace.
Never has the word seemed so fresh and precious.
Have a cup of tea and rejoice.
Act as if armistice has already arrived.
Don't wait another minute.
Celebrate today.

    —Judy Hill, "Wage Peace"

May suffering ones be suffering free
And the fear struck fearless be.
May the grieving shed all grief—
And the sick find health relief.

    —Zen chant

There is a light in this world, a healing spirit more
powerful than any darkness may encounter. We
sometimes lose sight of this force when there is suffering, too much pain. Then suddenly the spirit will

emerge through the lives of ordinary people who hear a call and answer in extraordinary ways.

—Mother Teresa

To love is to be responsible . . . in everything: the work we do, the things we buy, the food we eat, the people we look up to, the movies we see, the words we use, every choice we make from morning till night. That is the real measure of love; it is a wonderfully demanding responsibility.

—Eknath Easwaran

Mother of gods, father of gods,
Ancient God,
A mere appendage of the realm,
a common man, has come.
He comes crying, he comes in sadness,
he comes with guilt.
Perhaps he has slipped, perhaps he has stumbled,
perhaps he has touched the bird of evil, the spider's
    web, the tuft of thorns:
It wounds his heart, it troubles him.
Master, Lord,

Ever Present, Ever Near,
Take it from him: hear the pain of this common man.
   —Aztec prayer

Look down, Father of mercies, at those unhappy
families suffering from war and slaughter, from
hunger and illness and other severe troubles. Spare
them, O Lord, for it is truly a time of mercy. Amen.
   —Saint Peter Canisius

Why stand we here trembling around
Calling on God for help, and not ourselves, in
   whom God dwells,
Stretching a hand to save the falling man?
   —William Blake

Each time a man stands up for an ideal, or acts to
improve the lot of others, or strikes out against
injustice, he sends forth a tiny ripple of hope . . .
those ripples build a current that can sweep down
the mightiest walls of oppression and resistance.
   —Robert F. Kennedy

May all beings everywhere plagued
with sufferings of body and mind
quickly be freed from their illnesses.

May those frightened cease to be afraid,
and may those bound be free.

May the powerless find power,
and may people think of befriending one another.

May those who find themselves in trackless, fearful
    wilderness—
the children, the aged, the unprotected—
be guarded by beneficial celestials,
and may they swiftly attain enlightenment.
    —Buddhist salutation for peace

Hope . . . is not the same as joy that things are
going well, or willingness to invest in enterprises
that are obviously heading for . . . success, but
rather an ability to work for something because
it is good.
    —Vaclav Havel

A strange breed of monks, these 12,000 derelicts of
    life,
These lovable genial isolated human beings
They live with a past not to be forgotten,
A present built out of isolation,
And a future that promises and hopes for nothing.
These monks of the inner city are more alone
Than the strictest contemplative . . .
And often more redeemed
As they traffic in their currency of cigarettes,
Where to get beer, a bed, a meal, a job and some-
    times money,
They are selfless and concerned.
These islands of humanity boasting of a day's work.

And regretting a wasted life.

They trust no one as they walk.
Their silent world of pain and fear,
This order of the street, men without futures, with-
    out rights.
Poor, pushed, passed by and possessed by those who
    provide beds and food,
Keeping them on one aimless treadmill of life.

They live without solutions,
With no one listening to what they say,
No one asking them to talk,
Inviting them to spill, to drain
The poison from their lives,
A poison that festers in nightmares, alcohol,
Fear of work, passive acceptance of mistreatment,
  unexpressed anger and fear.

    —James Conlon, "The Monks of Skid Row"

It's a matter of taking the side of the weak against
the strong, something the best people have always
done.

    —Harriet Beecher Stowe

Lord, make me
an instrument of your peace;
where there is hatred,
let me sow love;
where there is injury,
pardon;
where there is doubt,
faith;
where there is despair,

hope;
where there is darkness,
light;
where there is sadness,
joy.
O Divine Master, grant that I may
not so much seek to be consoled,
as to console;
to be understood, as to
understand;
to be loved, as to
love.

—Saint Francis of Assisi

Every man must be his own leader. He now knows enough not to follow other people.

He must follow the light that's within himself, and through this light he will create a new community. . . .

I am aware of the fact that there are already people in existence today—take us—who really belong to a community which does not exist yet. That is, we are the bridge between the community we've left and the community which doesn't exist yet.

—Laurens van der Post

Almighty God, grant that I may awake to the joy of this day, finding gladness in all its toil and difficulty and in its pleasure and success, in all its failures and sorrow; teach me to throw open the windows of my life, that I may look always away from myself and behold the need of the world. Give me the will and strength to bring the gift of Thy gladness to others of Thy children, that with them I may stand to bear the burden and heat of the day and offer Thee the praise of work well done, through Jesus Christ our Lord. Amen.

—Author unknown

If I am not concerned for myself, who will be for me?
But if I am only concerned for myself, what good
    am I?
And if now is not the time to act, when will it be?

—Hillel

Do the thing and you will have the power.

—Ralph Waldo Emerson

The only answer in this life, to the loneliness we are all bound to feel, is community. The living together, working together, sharing together, loving God and loving our brother, and living close to him in community so we can show our love for Him.

—Dorothy Day

Black snow fell over Sarajevo,
darkening the mid-day sky with ashes
from the million and a half books burning
in what was once the national library.
The old librarian raced through shell-pocked streets,
his face reddening from the torrid heat pouring
out of the knot of smoking ruins where
he had spent a lifetime rescuing words
from oblivion. Defying the withering fire of the
    snipers,
he stood on the steps of the smoldering building
wanting to save—something, anything—even
the single sheet of cindered paper that drifted
    towards him
through the singed air, still holding fire from the
    inferno.

Catching the paper, which glowed in his hand
like a black and white negative held up
to the red light inside a photographer's darkroom,
he glared at what was once a page from a holy book,
an illuminated manuscript, and couldn't smell the
    skin
of his fingertips burning as he tried reading from
    what seemed
to be the last page of the last book on earth.
With time on fire, history incinerated,
the brittle page flaked and flared, then
vanished, leaving blue and gold and red ash
on his cold, numb hands.
Staring into the fiery ruins, he wondered
when he could start rebuilding.

    —Phil Cousineau, "Memoricide"

Within a system which denies the existence of basic
human rights, fear tends to be the order of the day.
Yet even under the most crushing state machinery,
courage rises up again and again, for fear is not the
natural state of civilized man.

    —Aung San Suu Kyi

This is not
the age of information.

This is *not*
the age of information.

Forget the news,
and the radio,
and the blurred screen.

This is the time
of loaves
and fishes.

People are hungry,
and one good word is bread
for a thousand.

  —David Whyte, "Loaves and Fishes"

O Lord, strengthen and support, we entreat Thee,
all persons unjustly accused or underrated. Comfort
them by the ever-present thought that Thou knowest the whole truth and wilt, in Thine own good
time, make their righteousness as clear as the light.
Give them grace to pray for such as do them wrong,

and hear and bless them when they pray; for the
sake of Jesus Christ our Lord and Savior. Amen.

—Christina Rossetti

Each person has inside a basic decency and goodness. If he listens to it and acts on it, he is giving a
great deal of what it is the world needs most. It is
not complicated but it takes courage. It takes
courage for a person to listen to his own goodness
and act on it.

—Pablo Casals

Make me a blessing, Lord. Help me to assist those
needing help, to be a blessing to my fellowmen.
Instruct me when to speak and when to hold my
speech, when to be bold in giving and when to
withhold; and if I have not strength enough, then
give me strength.

Lord, make me love myself and be tender
toward all others. Let there be outpoured on me the
gentleness to bless all who have need of gentleness.
Give me a word, a touch to fill the lonely life, faith
for the ill, and courage to keep hearts up though
my own is feeling just as low. When men have bit-

ter things to meet and quail and would accept
defeat, then let me lift their eyes to see the vision of
Thy victory. Help me to help; help me to give the
wisdom and the will to live.

—James Dillet Freeman

May the God of justice and mercy unite us in compassionate solidarity with all those in need, that our
lives may be just and merciful, and a source of Her
blessing to many.

—Marchiene Vroon Rienstra

I am a mother
Unconditional love
Reflecting you
Reflecting me
Reflecting you

I want my children to know love
To learn love
To be wrapped in love

My children are
Reflecting you

Reflecting them
Reflecting you

We are all impoverished
When stuck in the choice of two
When this or that is all we do

Give me another choice
This or that isn't enough for me

Give me another choice
I like the number three

Give me another choice
Black and white imprison my soul

Give me another choice
Infinite as a rainbow

Give me another choice
140 murders in Oakland
in the first two months of 2007

Give me another choice
102 American soldiers died in Iraq
in the first two months of 2007

Give me another choice
Military recruitment at school
Violence on the street

Give me another choice
I like the number three
 —Donna Chan, "I Like the Number 3"

Our responding to life's unfairness with sympathy
and with righteous indignation, God's compassion
and God's anger working through us, may be the
surest proof of all of God's reality.
 —Harold Kushner

How would it be
if just for today
we thought less about contests and rivalries,
profits and politics,
winners and sinners,
and more about
helping and giving,
mending and blending,

reaching out
and pitching in?

How would it be?

—Author unknown

The past is death's, the future is thine own. Take it
while it is still yours, and fix your mind, not on
what you may have done long ago to hurt, but on
what you can now do to help.

—Percy Bysshe Shelley

Lord, remember all those
Who feel tempted to suicide
And give them a reason to live.
Even if it is the wrong reason,
It can be changed later.
Finally Lord, I thank you that
You see the whole picture.
Teach us not to judge on just a part.

—Author unknown

Action is the antidote to despair.
—Joan Baez

You cannot hope to build a better world without improving the individuals. To that end each of us must work for his own improvement, and at the same time share a general responsibility for all humanity, our particular duty being to aid those to whom we think we can be most useful.
—Marie Curie

Nobody made a greater mistake than he who did nothing because he could only do a little.
—Edmund Burke

We cannot change the whole world. We cannot make everyone's situation what we perhaps would like it to be. But if we just try, one life at a time, to show others that there is hope, that others do care, perhaps the world will change around us in ways that we may not ever see, or truly understand. Improving the human condition one life at a time: This is our story of hope.
—Author unknown

Through a flower's flow of colors
And autumn wind's undone
And the still white of the winter
Under a sharp and glinting sun;

Through a meal with good old friends
All with family heartily bound
And the stories by the campfire
And songs that are pass'd 'round;

Through the smells of summer grasses,
Through the Redwood dells a' dawn,
After moonless nights, a' sunrise,
Where to gleaming shores we've gone;

Through the words we banter daily,
The common office jest,
Through the phrases that we know by,
That language we speak best;

Through the hearts on fire—and winging,
Through the thoughts that wing o'er the swell,
Through the spirit that comes unto us,
We know we're one as well.

The community of the heart brings one
On tender, on above
To present the present to us
In the quietest ways of love

The quietest way,
The quietest ways,
In the quietest way
Of love:

With each breath we breathe
In each moment that we last,
Before our eyes, in an eye's blink,
We make the future and the past!

And so it happens that each day,
Whether by chance or through an old song,
Opportunity will knock as you go—
To pass life's tune along.

> —Daniel Brady, "The Manifold Manners of
> Means: (Life's Tune)"

No man is an Island, entire of itself; every man is a
piece of Continent, a part of the main, if a clod be
washed away by the sea, Europe is the less, as well

as if a promontory were, as well as if a manor or thy
friends or of thine own were; any man's death
diminishes me, because I am involved in Mankind.

—John Donne

O Lord our God,
Who has bidden the light
To shine out of darkness,
Who hast again awakened us
To praise Thy goodness
And ask for Thy grace:
Accept now, in Thy endless mercy,
The sacrifice of our worship
And thanksgiving;

And grant unto us all such requests
As may be wholesome for us.
Make us to be children of the light
And of the day, and heirs
Of Thy everlasting inheritance.

Remember, O Lord,
According to the multitude of Thy mercies,
Thy whole Church:
All who join with us in prayer;
All our brethren by land or sea,

Or wherever they may be
In Thy vast Kingdom, who stand in need
Of Thy grace and succor.

Pour out upon them the riches
Of Thy mercy, so that we,
Redeemed in soul and body,
And steadfast in faith,
May ever praise Thy wonderful
And holy name. Amen.

   —Author unknown

There is no need to go searching for a remedy for
the evils of the time. The remedy already exists—
it is the gift of one's self to those who have fallen
so low that even hope fails them. Open wide your
heart.

   —Rene Bazin

All your strength is in your union;
All your danger in discord
Therefore be at peace henceforward
And as brothers live together.

   —Henry Wadsworth Longfellow

Blessed are all your saints, our God and King, who have traveled over life's tempestuous sea, and have arrived in the harbor of peace and felicity. Watch over us who are still in our dangerous voyage; and remember those who lie exposed to the rough storms of trouble and temptations. Frail is our vessel, and the ocean is wide; but as in your mercy you have set our course, so steer the vessel of our life toward the everlasting shore of peace, and bring us at length to the quiet haven of our heart's desire, where you, O our God, are blessed, and live and reign for ever and ever.

—Saint Augustine of Hippo

A lost child crying
Stumbling over the dark fields . . .
Catching fireflies
—Ryusui

There is no trust more sacred than the one the world holds with children. There is no duty more important than ensuring that their rights are respected, that their welfare is protected, that their lives are free from fear and want and that they grow up in peace.

—Kofi A. Annan

We wait in the darkness!
Come, all you who listen.
Help in our night journey:
Now no sun is shining;
Now no star is glowing.
Come show us the pathway:
The night is not friendly;
She closes her eyelids.
The moon did forget us,
We wait in the darkness!

—Iroquois song

Never despair. But if you do, work on in despair.

—Edmund Burke

This is the true joy in life, the being used for a purpose recognized by yourself as a mighty one . . . the being a force of Nature instead of a feverish selfish little clod of ailments and grievances complaining that the world will not devote itself to making you happy.

—George Bernard Shaw

Life's most persistent and urgent question is, "What are you doing for others?"

—Martin Luther King Jr.

Higher Power
As I may pass through the world but once:
any good therefore that I can do
or any kindness that I can show to another living being,
let me do so now;
let me not defer or neglect it,
for I may not pass this way again.
Amen.

—Author unknown

We have a call to do good, as often as we have the power and the occasion.

 —William Penn

Do what you can—and the task will rest lightly in your hand, so lightly that you will be able to look forward to the more difficult tests which may be awaiting you.

 —Dag Hammarskjöld

And now, may kindly Columba guide you
To be an isle in the sea,
To be a hill on the shore,
To be a star in the night,
To be a staff for the weak.
Amen.

 —Celtic prayer

Cultures develop from the integrity of the innumerable lived details that underlie what is believed, taught, enacted, from the art created and the ways all beings are treated. At this time in human history, each individual's original, daily, on-going contributions and commitment are critical.

—Deena Metzger

I don't say follow your bliss; look where that has gotten us. I say follow your heartbreak.

—Andrew Harvey

An individual must not wait for governments and he must not wait for groups and powerful people to do something. He must take care of what is on his doorstep. . . . You do what is necessary at a given moment with all your heart and all your soul.

—Laurens van der Post

Be kind and merciful. Let no one ever come to you without leaving better and happier. Be the living expression of God's kindness: kindness in your face, kindness in your smile, kindness in your warm greeting. In the slums we are the light of God's kindness to the poor. To children, to the poor, to all

who suffer and are lonely, give always a happy
smile. Give them not only your care, but also your
heart.

—Mother Teresa

May this be for me a day of blessing and peace.
May it be a day of safety and well-being.
May the rising sun infuse me with inspiration and
    hope.
    May my mind be filled with light.
May I give and receive only kindness.
May I accept and offer only healing.
May I come to know a deeper level of happiness,
    and may I move nearer today to true awakening.

May this be for you a day of blessing and peace.
May it be a day of safety and well-being.
May the rising sun infuse you with inspiration and
    hope.
    May your mind be filled with light.
May you give and receive only kindness.
May you accept and offer only healing.
May you come to know a deeper level of happiness,
    and may you move nearer today to true
        awakening.

May this be for all beings a day of blessing and peace.
May it be a day of safety and well-being.
May the rising sun infuse us all with inspiration
and hope.
May every mind be filled with light.
May we give and receive only kindness.
May we accept and offer only healing.
May all beings come to know a deeper level of
happiness,
and may we all move nearer today to true
awakening.

—Diane Berke, "A Prayer for the Dawn"

Do not believe that all greatness and heroism are in
the past. Learn to discover princes, prophets, heroes
and saints among the people about you. Be assured
they are there.

—Thomas Davidson

Loving God, you show yourself to those who are
vulnerable and make your home with the poor
and weak of this world;
Warm our hearts with the fire of your Spirit. Help
us to accept the challenge of AIDS.

Protect the healthy, we pray, calm the frightened,
    give courage to those in pain, comfort the dying
    and give to the dead eternal life.
Console the bereaved, we beg you, and strengthen
    those who care for the sick.
May we, your people, using all our energy and
    imagination, and trusting in your steadfast
    love, be united with one another in conquering
    all disease and fear.

—Author unknown

A commitment to love and justice demands the
transformation of social structures as well as of
hearts.

—Mary E. Hunt

My life belongs to the whole community, and as
long as I live, it is my privilege to do for it whatso-
ever I can. I want to be thoroughly used up when I
die, for the harder I work, the more I live. I rejoice
in life for its own sake. Life is no "brief candle" to
me. It is a sort of splendid torch which I have got
hold of for the moment, and I want to make it burn

as brightly as possible before handing it on to future
generations.
    —George Bernard Shaw

Everything that is done in the world is done by hope.
    —Martin Luther

You have been telling the people that this is the
    Eleventh Hour.
Now you must go back and tell the people that this
    is the hour.
And there are things to be considered:
Where are you living?
What are you doing?
What are your relationships?
Are you in right relation?
Where is your water?
Know your garden.
It is time to speak your Truth.
Create your community.
Be good to each other.
And do not look outside yourself for the leader.
Then he clasped his hands together, smiled, and said,
"This could be a good time!"

There is a river flowing now very fast.
It is so great and swift that there are those who will
    be afraid.
They will try to hold on to the shore.
They will feel they are being torn apart and will
    suffer greatly.
Know the river has its destination.
The elders say we must let go of the shore, push
    off into the middle
of the river, keep our eyes open and our heads
    above the water.
And I say, see who is in there with you and
    celebrate.
At this time in history we are to take nothing
    personally,
least of all, ourselves.
For the moment we do,
our spiritual growth and journey comes to a halt.
The time of the lone wolf is over.
Gather yourselves!
Banish the word struggle from your attitude
and your vocabulary.
All that we do now must be done in a sacred manner
and in celebration.
We are the ones we have been waiting for.

    —Author unknown, "A Hopi Elder Speaks"

Pity may represent little more than the impersonal
concern which prompts the mailing of a check,
but true sympathy is the personal concern which
demands the giving of one's soul.

—Martin Luther King Jr.

When cataclysm strikes, the spirit is tested.
    The Earth has turned in its sleep.
People have been crushed, killed, wounded.
    Let us pray for the survivors,
        that their lives may be rebuilt.

When cataclysm strikes, the spirit is tested,
    wakes from its dream of immortality.
Yet the spirit cannot be crushed, killed, wounded.
Let us pray that everyone who has suffered
    finds strength in the spirit.

—Author unknown

Charity begins today.
Today somebody is suffering,
today somebody is in the street,
today somebody is hungry.
Our work is for today;

yesterday has gone,
tomorrow has not yet come.

—Mother Teresa

When people ask me "Where is God?" I tell them
I would rather rephrase the question to—"When is
God?" Encountering God is not a matter of being
in the right place, but of doing the right thing. God
comes into our lives when we do things that make
us truly human. When we help the poor, when we
speak out for justice, when we get over our exagger-
ated sense of our own importance, when we learn
to respond with child-like awe . . . we make room
in our lives for God.

—Harold Kushner

Loving God,
lead us beyond ourselves
to care and protect,
to nourish and shape,
to challenge and energize
both the life and the world
You have given us.

God of light and God of darkness,
God of conscience and God of courage
lead us through this time
of spiritual confusion and public uncertainty.

Lead us beyond fear, apathy and defensiveness
to new hope in You and to hearts full of faith.

Give us the conscience it takes
to comprehend what we're facing,
to see what we're looking at
and to say what we see
so that others, hearing us,
may also brave the pressure that comes
with being out of public step.

Give us the courage we need
to confront those things
that compromise our consciences
or threaten our integrity.

Give us, most of all,
the courage to follow those before us
who challenged wrong
and changed it,
whatever the cost to themselves.

Mary, Mother of Jesus,
you confronted the systems
of the world
in order to do the will of God.
Touch our conscience
on behalf of those burdened
by oppressive laws
and give us courage
to join them in the struggle.

St. Marguerite Bourgeoys,
founder of the Congregation of Notre Dame,
you challenged even the church
in order to send women missionaries
into foreign lands.
Touch our conscience
on behalf of women everywhere
and give us courage to support them.

St. Thomas Aquinas,
doctor of the church,
you were condemned
by the bishop of Paris
for reconciling the theology of the time
with the thinking of the time.
Touch our conscience
on behalf of new ideas
and give us courage to test them.

St. Maximilian Kolbe,
you gave your life
in place of a condemned prisoner
in Auschwitz.
Touch our conscience
on behalf of life
and give us the courage
to protect it.

St. Polycarp,
you were executed for refusing
to proclaim "Caesar is Lord."
Touch our conscience
on behalf of just government
and give us the courage to demand it.

St. Joan of Arc,
you were burned at the stake as a heretic
by the church itself
for refusing to betray
the voice of God in you.
Touch our conscience
on behalf of the visionaries
in church and society
and give us the courage
to share their risk.

St. Basil the Great,
doctor of the church,
you challenged the wealthy
to redistribute their wealth to the poor.
Touch our conscience
on behalf of those who are paid unjust wages
and give us the courage
to proclaim that cause.

Shiphrah and Puah,
you saved the life of the child Moses
by breaking the law of the land.
Touch our conscience
on the subject of unjust laws
and give us the courage to protest them.

St. Stanislaus, Bishop of Krakow,
You denounced the abuses of the king.
Touch our conscience
with an awareness of civil abuse
and give us the courage to confront it.

St. John the Baptist,
you were beheaded
for speaking truth to power.
Touch our conscience
on behalf of immoral public policy
and give us the courage to speak our truth.

St. Teresa of Avila,
doctor of the church,
you were under suspicion
by the Spanish Inquisition
for developing a new form of spirituality.
Touch our conscience
on behalf of those who break new paths
and give us the courage always
to embrace new ways
for the good of the world.

St. Hildegard of Bingen,
Benedictine abbess,
you claimed your own authority
despite ecclesiastical interdict.
Touch our conscience
on behalf of the forgotten
and give us the courage
to assert the rights of those
abandoned by the system.

St. Hugh,
Bishop of Lincoln, England,
you practiced tax evasion
in an attempt to deny the king money
to launch a crusade.
Touch our conscience

about the national budget
and give us the courage to critique it publicly.

Holy Pope John XXIII,
you opened the church to the modern world.
Touch our conscience
on behalf of new ideas,
in support of new understandings,
and give us the courage to risk them.

Holy Sister Juana Inés de la Cruz,
you were criticized for writing
the first theological work by a woman.
Touch our conscience
in regard to the role of women
in church and societies,
and give us the courage to promote their rights.

Holy Mary Ward,
founder of the Institute of the Blessed Virgin Mary,
you were arrested by Rome and declared heretic
for founding a women's religious order
unenclosed and free of episcopal control.
Touch our conscience
on behalf of the full authority of women
and give us the courage to live it.

Holy Mohandas Gandhi,
you freed India from English jurisdiction
through nonviolent resistance.
Touch our conscience
on behalf of the oppressed of the world
and give us the courage to resist oppression
in ways that are not themselves oppressive.

Holy Cesar Chavez,
farmworker and organizer,
you organized migrant workers
to struggle for just wages
through boycotts and civil disobedience.
Touch our conscience
on behalf of workers' rights
and give us the courage to strive for them.

Holy John Howard Griffin,
author, you made yourself black
in order to expose the horrors of racism.
Touch our conscience
on behalf of the marginalized
and give us the courage
to embrace their cause.

Holy Maura Clarke
and Companions,

you were brutally murdered in El Salvador
for supporting refugee priests, people and catechists
in their struggle against an oppressive government.
Touch our conscience
on behalf of the oppressed in both state and church,
and give us the courage to join them
in the struggle.

Holy Stephen Biko,
you devoted yourself to raising consciousness
in apartheid South Africa
and died for the doing of it.
Touch our conscience
on behalf of hard truths
and give us the courage
to pursue them
whatever the cost to ourselves.

Holy Philip Berrigan,
you spent half a lifetime
in prison to protest the nuclear policies
of the United States.
Touch our conscience as citizens of the globe
and give us the courage to give our lives
to making life better, safer, more human
for the rest of humankind.

Finally, Great God,
give us the kind of faith in you
that was the mainstay
of those before us
who followed you from
Galilee to Jerusalem
doing good,
raising the dead to life
and singing alleluia all the way.

God of Conscience, God of Courage
give us whatever grace we need
to work for the coming
of the reign of God
now, here and always.
Amen.

> —Joan Chittister, OSB, "Prayer for Conscience
> and Courage in Times of Public Struggle"

Prayers for Our World

The golden invitation of the twenty-first century is
for us to bring our great dreams forward and collectively join in our common work of fostering a great
dream: What world could we create together, by
dreaming together collectively, that could work for
everyone? Because essentially that's what we want.
That's why we've been so mysteriously placed on
this great blue jewel called Earth.

—Angeles Arrien

I talk about it sometimes with Him, all the suffering in the world.

"Dear God," I have prayed, "how is it possible
all the horrors I have seen, all the atrocities you
allow man

to commit when you—God—are ever standing
so near and could help us?
Could we not hear your voice say 'No'
with such love and power
never again would
we harm?"

And my Lord replied, "Who would understand
        if I said that I
cannot bear
to confine a wing, and not let it learn from the
        course it chooses."

But what of a man walking lost in a forest
weeping and calling your name for help, and
        unknown to him he
is heading for a covered pit with sharp spears in it
that will maim his flesh when he crashes
through the trap?

"Yes, why don't I remove every object from this
        world that could
cause someone to weep? Yes, why don't I speak
        in a way
that could save a life?

I opened up my hand and the Infinite ran to the
        edges of space—

and all possibilities are contained therein, all
    possibilities,
even sorrow.

In the end, nothing that ever caused one pain
    will exist.
No one will begrudge Me.

The Absolute Innocence of all within my Creation
    takes a while to understand."

    —Saint Catherine of Siena, "No One Will
      Begrudge Me"
    Translated by Daniel Ladinsky

May there be peace on earth, peace in the
    atmosphere,
and in the heavens. Peaceful be the waters, the
    herbs, and plants.
May the Divine bring us peace.
May the holy prayers and invocations of peace-
    liturgies generate ultimate peace
and Happiness everywhere.
With these meditations, which resolve and dissolve
    harm, violence, and conflicts,
we render peaceful whatever on earth is terrible,
    sinful, cruel, and violent.

Let the earth become fully auspicious, let everything
be beneficial to us.

    —Atharva Veda, XIX-9

Help us, O Lord, to remember our kindred beyond
the sea—all those who bend in bonds, of our own
blood and of human kind—the lowly and the
wretched, the ignorant and the weak. We are one
world . . . and one great human problem and what
we do here goes to solve not only our petty troubles
alone but the difficulties and desires of millions
unborn and unknown. Let us then realize our
responsibilities and gain strength to bear them
worthily.

    —W. E. B. Du Bois

Lead me from death to life,
From falsehood to truth.
Lead me from despair to hope,
From fear to trust.
Lead me from hate to love,
From war to peace.

Let peace fill our hearts,
our world, our universe.
Amen.

   —Universal Prayer for Peace

O Lord, we bring before you the distress and dangers of peoples and nations, the pleas of the imprisoned and the captive, the sorrows of the grief-stricken, the needs of the refugee, the impotence of the weak, the weariness of the despondent, and the diminishments of the aging. O Lord, stay close to all of them. Amen.

   —Saint Anselm

To put the world in order we must first
put the nation in order.
To put the nation in order we must first
put the family in order.
To put the family in order we must first
cultivate our personal life.
And to cultivate our personal life,
we must set our hearts right.

   —Confucius

He was elderly
That's what you'd call him
Still pretty tall, frail though
He had to be in his 80's
I happened to be there
And watched him walk steadily
Going toward The Wall
It was winter then
The cold white light peculiar to that season
Glowed upon him
And made his white hair,
Close cropped and thinning as it was
All the brighter
He wore a blue woolen suit
And a veteran's cap
Tied to the point at its back
Were a set of feathers
It had been these
And their dangling strings attaching them
That had caught my eye, at first

He went along a direct line
As he approached The Wall
Honoring the Vietnam War's dead
And so seemed to know

The exact point of his destination
He'd been there before

Knowing

And he stopped, of course
Before it and drew himself up
Took off his spectacles
Wiped them and placed them back on

I was on my own pilgrimage
And by then was not far behind him
To his left

I did not mean to intrude
So I hesitated, a moment
Even as he seemed to
And took precautions
To keep my shadow out of his sight
Instead of moving on though, I remained
Curious

He raised his hand and extended it slowly
To The Wall

The sunset colors warmed its polished surface
And I watched his hand's shadow approach the
    real deal

As reality and reflection met
He sadly looked down
Not at any particular name, I could see that
But staring, somehow away
Into time
Into some place I'll never know

I heard him sigh
Noticed his lips in the barest of motions
Then, in a moment of quietude, I heard his
    murmur

Saw that he hadn't placed his hand on any one
    name
And that he moved it along to a few places
As if searching, blindly for something
I felt he was addressing them all
That this was his personal and intimately mute
    wailing wall
I stepped away—I did not belong in his service

Was he one of the "old men" of that war?
Who is he hoping to touch?
What laughter was he hearing?
Whose smile does he miss still?
After all these years . . .

I, on the other hand,
Had my own meaning to find from The Wall
My own ghosts to address

When he walked away
He went more slowly than when he'd come
And seemed a bit more stooped maybe

When he'd gone about twenty paces
He stopped, removed his glasses
Wiped them
Took a deep breath and looked beyond to the
    capital's dome
Before moving on

That's when I turned to face the wall
I touched it too
For my brother
For all the brothers
And the sorrow that yet breaks me down
From time to time
When a song plays
When a headline reads
When I am reminded of an immense lie
And how, tears serve, when nothing else does
To honor those who believed
That their sacrifice was worth its value

    —Daniel Brady, "Hand to Hand"

We must concentrate not merely on the negative expulsion of war but the positive affirmation of peace.

—Martin Luther King Jr.

Come Holy Spirit, breathe down upon our troubled
    world.
Shake the tired foundations of our crumbling
    institutions.
Break the rules that keep you out of all our sacred
    spaces,
and from the dust and rubble, gather up the
    seedlings of a new creation.

Come Holy Spirit, enflame once more the dying
    embers of our weariness.
Shake us out of our complacency. Whisper our
    names once more,
and scatter your gifts of grace with wild abandon.
Break open the prisons of our inner being,
and let your raging justice be our sign of liberty.

Come Holy Spirit and lead us to places we would
    rather not go.

Expand the horizons of our limited imaginations.
Awaken in our souls dangerous dreams for a new
    tomorrow,
and rekindle in our hearts the fire of prophetic
    enthusiasm.

Come Holy Spirit, whose justice outwits interna-
    tional conspiracy,
whose light outshines religious bigotry,
whose peace can halt our patriarchal hunger for
    dominance and control,
whose promise invigorates out every effort:
to create a new heaven and a new earth, now and
    forever. Amen.

    —Diarmuid O'Murchu, "Prayer to the Holy
      Spirit"

In spite of everything I still believe that people are
really good at heart. I simply can't build up my
hopes on a foundation consisting of confusion,
misery and death. . . . Yet, if I look up into the
heavens, I think that it will all come right, that this
cruelty too will end, and that peace and tranquility
will return again.

    —Anne Frank

"Tell me the weight of a snowflake," a robin asked a wild dove.

"Nothing more than nothing," was the answer.

"In that case I must tell you a marvelous story," the robin said. "I sat on the branch of a fir, close to its trunk, when it began to snow—not heavily, not in a raging blizzard, no, just like in a dream, without any violence. Since I didn't have anything better to do, I counted the snowflakes settling on the twigs and needles of my branch. The number was exactly 3,741,952. When the next snowflake dropped onto the branch—nothing more than nothing, as you say—the branch broke off." Having said that, the robin flew away.

The dove, since Noah's time an authority on the matter, thought about the story for awhile and finally said to herself: "Perhaps there is only one person's voice lacking for peace to come about in the world."

—Author unknown

The force of arms cannot do what peace does. If you can gain your desired end with sugar, why use poison?

—Somadeva

O God, we seek your forgiveness for the numerous
      injustices around us,
    for our inability to create a world of equality.
We pray for a deepening of our commitment to
      justice,
    for the ability to reflect on the many ways in
      which
    we offend people of other creeds, of the oppo-
      site sex, of other nations.
Above all we ask for the courage to stand up as
      witness-bearers for justice,
    though this may be against ourselves.
    —Unitarian Universalist prayer

What is the use of living if not to strive for noble
causes and to make this muddled world a better
place for those who will live in it after we are gone.
    —Winston Churchill

Great Spirit, you have been here always, and before
you, nothing has been. There is no one to pray to
but you. The star nations throughout the heavens

are yours, and yours are the green grasses of the earth mother. You are older than all need, older than all pain, older than all prayer.

Great Spirit, all over the world the faces of living ones are alike. With tenderness, they have come up out of the ground. Grandfather, look upon your grandchildren, with children in their arms, that they may face the winds and walk the good road to the day of silence.

Great Spirit, fill us with the light. Give us the strength to understand and the eyes to see. Teach us how to walk the soft earth as relatives to all living beings. Help us, O Grandfather, for without you we are nothing.

—Sioux prayer

Just as the rivers are much less numerous than the underground streams, so the idealism that is visible is minor compared to what men and women carry in their hearts, unreleased and scarcely released. Mankind is waiting and longing for those who can accomplish the task of untying what is knotted and bringing the underground waters to the surface.

—Albert Schweitzer

Mothers and wives, 'tis the call to arms
That the bugler yonder prepares to sound;
We stand on the brink of war's alarms
And your men may lie on a bloodstained ground.
The drums may play and the flags may fly,
And our boys may don the brown and blue,
And the call that summons brave men to die
Is the call for glorious women, too.

Mothers and wives, if the summons comes,
You, as ever since war has been,
Must hear with courage the rolling drums
And dry your tears when the flags are seen.
For never has hero fought and died
Who has braver been than the mother, who
Buckled his saber at his side,
And sent him forward to dare and do.

Mothers and wives, should the call ring out,
It is you must answer your country's cry:
You must furnish brave hearts and stout
For the firing line where the heroes die.
And never a corpse on the field of strife
Should be honored more in his country's sight
Than the noble mother or noble wife
Who sent him forth in the cause of right.

Mothers and wives, 'tis the call for men
To give their strength and to give their lives;
But well we know, such a summons then
Is the call for mothers and loyal wives.
For you must give us the strength we need,
You must give us the boys in blue,
For never a boy or a man shall bleed
But a mother or wife shall suffer, too.

—Edgar A. Guest (written in 1918)

It is only the women whose eyes have been washed
clear with tears who get the broad vision that makes
them little sisters to all the world.

—Dorothy Dix

From the voice of a devastated Earth a voice goes
        up with
Our own. It says: "Disarm! Disarm!
The sword of murder is not the balance of justice."
Blood does not wipe our dishonor,
Nor violence indicate possession.
As men have often forsaken the plough and the
        anvil
At the summons of war,

Let women now leave all that may be left of home
For a great and earnest day of counsel.
Let them meet first, as women, to bewail and
    commemorate the dead.
Let them solemnly take counsel with each other
    as to the means
Whereby the great human family can live in peace. . . .

    —Julia Ward Howe, from the Mother's Day
    Proclamation, 1870

Christ has no body now on earth but yours;
Yours are the only hands with which he can do
    his work,
Yours are the only feet with which he can go about
    the world,
Yours are the only eyes through which his com-
    passion
    Can shine forth upon a troubled world.
Christ has no body on earth now but yours.

    —Saint Teresa of Avila

Our loyalties must transcend our race, our tribe,
our class, and our nation; and this means we must
develop a world perspective.

    —Martin Luther King Jr.

May beings all live happily and safe
And may their hearts rejoice within themselves.
Whatever there may be with breath of life,
Whether they be frail or very strong,
Without exception, be they long or short
Or middle-sized, or be they big or small,
Or thick, or visible, or invisible,
Or whether they dwell far or they dwell near,
Those that are here, those seeking to exist—
May beings all rejoice within themselves.
Let no one bring about another's ruin
And not despise in any way or place,
Let them not wish each other any ill
From provocation or from enmity.

    —The Buddha, *Sutta Nipata*

The clear sky,
The green fruitful earth is good;
But peace among men is better.

    —Omaha song

We cannot merely pray to You, O God, to
    banish war,
For You have filled the world with paths to peace,
If only we would take them

We cannot merely pray for prejudice to cease,
For we might see the good in all
That lies right before our eyes,
If only we would use them.

We cannot merely pray to You to end starvation:
For there is food enough for all,
If only we would share it.

We cannot merely pray to You: "Root out despair,"
For the spark of hope already waits in the
    human heart
For us to fan it into flame.

We must not ask of You, O God,
That you take the task You have given to us.
We cannot shirk. We cannot flee away,
Avoiding our sacred obligation forever.

Therefore we pray, O God,
For wisdom and will,
For courage to do and to become,

Not merely to gaze with helpless yearning
As though we had no strength.
So that our land, our world, may be safe,
And our lives truly be blessed.

   —From the Jewish Liberal Prayerbook (United
     Kingdom)

Perhaps in His wisdom the Almighty is trying to
show us that a leader may chart the way, may point
out the road to lasting peace, but that many leaders
and many peoples must do the building.

   —Eleanor Roosevelt

FOR LILIANA URSU

Have you heard about the list of seventy-two
      banned words?
During the benighted '80s the Ceaucescu
      government
Compiled an official list of forbidden words,
Topped off by a steeple of religious terms,
Such as *God, angel, church,* and *cross.*

Not coincidentally, the authorities imprisoned
      dirty words

In the dank crypt of their list, and secreted away
The endarkened ones, like despair,
Anxiety, sadness, and *depression.*

"They amputated the language," the exiled poet
    later reported.
"You spoke freely at home, but of course the phones
    were bugged.
We joked at the Writer's Union not to spill any
    drinks.
The hidden microphones would get rusty."

The Romanian people lived like schizophrenics,
    she reveals,
Using one word, meaning another, torn apart by
    doubt in
The mutinous dark, wondering if their spies lurked
    in their own families.
Still they defied the censors by clinging to numinous
    words like
Heaven, melancholy, or *alone,* as if they were rafts
Clung to by shipwrecked sailors.

"At first *solitude* was also on the list,
But they changed their minds," the poet recalled,
    wistfully.
"My friends and I had a party celebrating
The release of the word *solitude.*"
    —Phil Cousineau, "Banned Words"

Lighting a candle is a prayer,
When we have gone, it stays alight,
kindling in the hearts and minds
of others the prayers we have
already offered for them
and for others, for the sad,
the sick, and the suffering—
the prayers of thankfulness too.

Lighting a candle is a parable:
burning itself out, it gives light to others.
Christ gave himself for others.
He calls us to give ourselves.

Lighting a candle is a symbol:
of love and hope,
of light and warmth.
Our world needs them all.

  —Author unknown

Love gives us the courage to believe in humanity
and in ourselves. . . . It takes courage to commit
yourself to building bridges between the world that

could be and the world that is—the courage to say
that you believe the world will one day be a better
place and that today you are ready to do your part
to make it so.

    —Laurence Boldt

In Singapore, in the airport,
a darkness was ripped from my eyes.
In the women's restroom, one compartment
    stood open.
A woman knelt there, washing something
    in the white bowl.

Disgust argued in my stomach
and I felt, in my pocket, for my ticket.

A poem should always have birds in it.
Kingfishers, say, with their bold eyes and gaudy
    wings.
Rivers are pleasant, and of course trees.
A waterfall, or if that's not possible, a fountain
    rising and falling.
A person wants to stand in a happy place, in a
    poem.

When the woman turned I could not answer
     her face.
Her beauty and her embarrassment struggled
     together, and
     neither could win.
She smiled and I smiled. What kind of nonsense
     is this?
Everybody needs a job.

Yes, a person wants to stand in a happy place, in
     a poem.
But first we must watch her as she stares down at
     her labor,
     which is dull enough.
She is washing the tops of the airport ashtrays, as
     big as
     hubcaps, with a blue rag.
Her small hands turn the metal, scrubbing and
     rinsing.
She does not work slowly, nor quickly, but like a
     river.
Her dark hair is like the wing of a bird.

I don't doubt for a moment that she loves her life.
And I want her to rise up from the crust and the slop
     and fly down to the river.
This probably won't happen.
But maybe it will.

If the world were only pain and logic, who would
    want it?

Of course, it isn't.
Neither do I mean anything miraculous, but only
the light that can shine out of a life. I mean
the way she unfolded and refolded the blue cloth,
the way her smile was only for my sake; I mean
the way this poem is filled with trees, and birds.

    —Mary Oliver, "Singapore"

We are not alone; beyond the differences that separate us, we share one common humanity and thus
belong to each other. The mystery of life is that we
discover this human togetherness not when we are
powerful and strong, but when we are vulnerable
and weak.

    —Henri J. M. Nouwen

May we unite in our minds,
Unite in our purposes and
Not fight against the divine spirit
Within us.

    —Atharva Veda

Great Spirit, Great Spirit, my Grandfather,
all over the earth the faces of living things are
      all alike.
With tenderness have these come up out of the
      ground.
Look upon these faces of children without number
      and with children in their arms,
that they may face the winds
and walk the good road to the day of quiet.
      —Black Elk

The . . . experience I'm talking about has given me
one certainty: . . . the salvation of this human world
lies nowhere else than in the human heart, in the
human power to reflect, in human meekness and in
human responsibility. Without a global revolution
in . . . human consciousness, nothing will change
for the better, and the catastrophe toward which
this world is headed . . . will be unavoidable.
      —Vaclav Havel

O God who art Peace everlasting, whose chosen
reward is the gift of peace, and who has taught us
that the peacemakers are Thy children, pour Thy
sweet peace into our souls, that everything discor-
dant may utterly vanish, and all that makes for
peace be sweet for us forever.

 —Galasian

Poverty is
a knee-level view from your bit of pavement;
a battered, upturned cooking pot and countable ribs,
coughing from your steel-banded lungs, alone, with
  your face to the wall;
shrunken breasts and a three year old who cannot
  stand
the ringed fingers, the eyes averted and a five-paise
  piece in your palm
smoking the babus' cigarette butts to quieten the
  fiend in your belly;
a husband without a job, without a square meal a
  day, without energy, without hope;
being at the mercy of everyone further up the lad-
  der because you are a threat to their self-respect;
a hut of tins and rags and plastic bags, in a warren
  of huts you cannot stand up in, where

your neighbors live at one arm's length across the
	lane;
a man who cries out in silence;
nobody listening, for everyone's talking;
the prayer withheld
the heart withheld
the hand withheld; yours and mine.

—Author unknown, written in Calcutta

I do not want to talk about what you understand
about this world. I want to know what you will
do about it. I do not want to know what you *hope*.
I want to know what you will *work for*. I do not
want your sympathy for the needs of humanity. I
want your *muscle*. As the wagon driver said when
they came to a long, hard hill, "Them that's going
on with us, get out and push. Them that ain't, get
out of the way."

—Robert Fulghum

If you don't like the way the world is, you change it.
You have an obligation to change it. You just do it
one step at a time.

—Marian Wright Edelman

I am done with great things, great institutions and big success, and I am for those tiny invisible molecular moral forces that work from individual to individual creeping through the crannies of the world like so many rootlets, or like the capillary oozing of water, yet which, if you give them time, will rend the hardest monuments of man's pride.

    —William James

I call myself a nationalist, but my nationalism is as broad as the universe. It includes in its sweep all the nations of the Earth. My nationalism includes the well-being of the whole world.

    —Mohandas Gandhi

Two horses
on the wide brow of the hill
and a woman with dark hair
looking toward me
as if she knew me.
Strange and familiar
this silent togetherness,

walking the horses on the
tawny heath.

Until she stops,
gathers herself
on that white
litheness and rides
toward the Black Mountains
brooding in the west.

I follow her until
we slow together
on the round
knoll, the silence
between us
like a third companion,
the clouds streaming
from us in a wide sky
and the mountains
framing her face.

My fortieth year,
and I think of time stopped
and time slipping by
and all the other faces
in all the other years
still looking and still waiting.

They come to us
flowering and fading
through a thousand forms.

And they do not wait
until we are ready.

I remember
the dark rippled cobbles
in an ancient square
and that broken
beggar's mouth
moving slowly,
as if to open.

That beautiful
breathless woman in blue
turning toward me
in sunlight,

and
that daughter
on the flatbed truck
beseeching for her wounded
father.

The world is full
of strangers
who demand our love
and deserve it.

For their mouths
loving or helpless.
For their eyes,
beautiful or not,

for their hair,
raven or mouse,
and their faces,
clear or clouded
by their past,

and most of all
like this one,
for her courage

who asked me
a stranger
to join her,

two familiars
who might never
meet again

their faces
in this moment
calm and protected
from suffering,

looking from the white
manes of their
stamping horses,

pilgrims of the
timeless and untravelled,
over the wide curve
of a trembling world.
    —David Whyte, "Two Strangers"

Walk together, talk together, O you people of the
    earth,
and then, only then, can you have peace.
    —Vedic teaching

If I had one prayer, I'd pray for people who hate
Maybe I'm out of my mind . . . or deep in my faith
A man grows old . . . when his soul's in pain
Only love can loosen that chain

But if I offer you grace, will it cause any change
And do I appear weak, if I calm my rage
I think of revenge, but will I become
The thing I despise, when a heart goes numb

I'll say a prayer, hoping it finds . . . people who hate
I send it now, to heal the hearts . . . of people who
    hate

If only one song . . . could silence hate
And end all the war . . . before it's too late
If a cold mind . . . could begin to feel
Then the fear in our world . . . has a chance to heal

I'll say a prayer, knowing it finds . . . people who
    hate
I send it now, to heal the hearts . . . of people who
    hate
. . . pray for people who hate
All of our thoughts . . . can set the stage
For the power of love . . . is larger than rage
When we take revenge . . . we will become
The hate we despise . . . as our soul goes numb

I have One Prayer . . . for the world to hear
It's a cry for mercy . . . the last of our tears

Let hate dissolve . . . let the past reveal
That love has shown us what is real

Angels above, quiet the pain . . . in people who hate
I'm sending One Prayer, to heal the hearts . . . in
      people who hate

One prayer . . . Pray!

(May all be loved, may all be blessed, may all feel
      peace . . . pray for people who hate)

I'm sending love to people who hate
I must be out of my mind . . . or deep in my faith
      —Karl Anthony, "One Prayer"

God is present in the confusion and dislocation of
the world. One encounters God not by turning
one's back on that world but by plunging into it
with the faith that the divine-human encounter
occurs in the midst of the encounter of human with
human, especially in the struggle to create signs of
the coming of God's reign of peace and justice.
      —Harvey Cox

O God,
Let us be united;
Let us speak in harmony;
Let our minds apprehend alike.
Common be our prayer;
Common be the end of our assembly;
Common be our resolution;
Common be our deliberations.
Alike be our feelings;
Unified be our hearts;
Common be our intentions;
Perfect be our unity.

 —Rig-Veda

If prayers are going to be answered at all, human beings probably have to answer them for each other.

 —Margaret Lee Runbeck

In future days, which we seek to make more secure, we look forward to a world founded upon four essential freedoms. The first is the freedom of speech and expression—everywhere in the world. The second is freedom of every person to worship God in his own way—everywhere in the world. The

third is freedom from want. . . . The fourth is freedom from fear.

—Franklin D. Roosevelt

For to be free is not merely to cast off one's chains,
but to live in a way that respects and enhances the
freedom of others.

—Nelson Mandela

O God of Mystery,
Who with great love, beauty and creativity
has established heaven and earth
by a single creative thought

O Source of all Love
Lover and inner presence
of all that is at this very moment
We thank you.

We are in a dangerous time, Great Mystery
We are in need of your grace and creativity.
All forms of life are being devalued and destroyed
Violence, meaningless sex and winning are glorified.
Your way and your gifts are taken for granted

O God of the Loving Gaze
These are dangerous times
We need a great work for our world.

You have sent your saints Helen and Marya
They tell us we are your saints.
We are to do a great work for these dangerous times.

They tell us to do something,
no matter how small
It will ripple and change the world
Because we are all connected.

O God of our connection
You are so wise and so creative.
Thank you for the way we touch one another.
Thank you for the way You touch our hearts.

My heart is ready to do my great work.
I will remind myself and those around me
Of the great work of creation You share with us
I will place great value on creating and the
    imagination

I will include creativity in my life
I will offer opportunities for and encouragement of
    creativity in others

I will remember the healing it offers to souls
I will be your cheerleader of the arts, with Your grace.

O Mystery of the Loving Gaze,
I am in awe of your artistry
And generosity in sharing creativity with us
Lead us to create a great work for our troubled
world.

> —Mary Peterson, "Psalm of the Great Work in
> Dangerous Times"

Almighty God, grant us grace fearlessly to contend
against evil, and to make no peace with oppression;
and, that we may reverently use our freedom, help
us to employ it in the maintenance of justice among
people and nations.

> —Adapted from The Book of Common Prayer

Dear Lord,
Creator of the world,
Help us love one another;
Help us care for one another
As sister or as brother.

May friendship grow
From nation to nation.
Bring peace to our world,
Dear Lord of Creation.

—Author unknown

I believe without a shadow of doubt that science
and peace will finally triumph over ignorance and
war, and that the nations of the earth will ultimately
agree not to destroy but to build up.

—Louis Pasteur

Grant, O merciful God, that with malice toward
none, with charity to all, with firmness in the right
as Thou givest us to see the right, we may strive to
finish the work we are in: to bind up the nation's
wounds; to care for him who shall have borne the
battle and for his widow and his orphan; to do all
which may achieve and cherish a just and lasting
peace among ourselves and with all nations. Amen.

—Abraham Lincoln

When God said, "My hands are yours," I saw that I
    could heal any
creature in this world;

I saw that the divine beauty in each heart
is the root of all time
and space.

I was once a sleeping ocean
and in a dream became
jealous of a
pond.

A penny can be eyed in the street
and a war can break out
over it amongst
the poor.

Until we know that God lives in us
and we can see Him
there,

a great poverty
we suffer.

    —Rabia, "Jealous of a Pond"
    Translated by Daniel Ladinsky

If we are to teach real peace in this world and if we are to carry on a real war against war, we shall have to begin with children; and if they will grow up in their natural innocence, we won't have to struggle; we won't have to pass fruitless, idle resolutions, but we shall go from love to love and peace to peace, until at last all the corners of the world are covered with that peace and love for which, consciously or unconsciously, the whole world is hungering.

—Mohandas Gandhi

Sacred journey, sacred story,
Truth we search for, truth we find.
Grace in the greening, beauty everywhere.
O come dream the dream of the earth.
O come dream the dream of the earth.

Path of communion, path of wonder,
Common heart and common home.
Grace in the oneness—brother, sister, star.
O come dream the dream of the earth
O come dream the dream of the earth

—Diane Forrest, OP, "The Dream of the Earth"

May the vision that so many mystic masters of all
traditions have had, of a future world free of cruelty
and horror, where humanity can live in the ultimate
happiness of the nature of mind, come, through all
our efforts, to be realized.

—Sogyal Rinpoche

War is the greatest plague that can afflict humanity;
it destroys religion, it destroys states, it destroys
families. Any scourge is preferable to it.

—Martin Luther

On your last days on earth
you promised
to leave us the Holy Spirit
as our present comforter.
We also know that your Holy Spirit blows over
    this earth.

But we do not understand him.
Many think
he is only wind or a feeling.

Let Your Holy Spirit
break into our lives.
Let him come like blood into our veins,
so that we will be driven
entirely by your will.
Let your Spirit
blow over wealthy Europe and America,
so that men there will be humble.
Let him blow over the poor parts of the world,
So that men there need suffer no more.
Let him blow over Africa,
so that men here may understand
what true freedom is.
There are a thousand voices and spirits
in this world,
but we want to hear only your voice,
and be open only to your Spirit.

 —African prayer

Self-love but serves the virtuous mind to wake,
As the small pebble stirs the peaceful lake;
The centre moved, a circle straight succeeds,
Another still and still another spreads;
Friend, parent, neighbor first it will embrace;
His country next; and next all human race.

 —Alexander Pope

There are those who are trying to set fire to the
    world,
We are in danger.
There is time only to work slowly,
There is no time not to love.

    —Deena Metzger, "Song"

Love is the light that dissolves all walls between
souls, families, and nations.

    —Paramahansa Yogananda

I add my breath to your breath
that our days be long on the Earth,
that the days of our people may be long,
that we shall be as one person,
that we may finish our road together.

    —Laguna Pueblo prayer

The teachings of all the great mystical paths of the
world make it clear that there is within us an enor-
mous reservoir of power, the power of wisdom and

compassion, the power of what Christ called the Kingdom of Heaven. If we learn how to use it . . . it can transform not only ourselves but the world around us. Has there ever been a time when the clear use of this sacred power was more essential or more urgent? Has there ever been a time when it was more vital to understand . . . how to use it for the sake of the world?

—Sogyal Rinpoche

With bended knees, with hands outstretched, do I yearn for the effective expression of the holy spirit working within me:

For this love and understanding, truth and justice; for wisdom to know the apparent from the real that I might alleviate the sufferings of men on earth . . .

God is love, understanding, wisdom, and virtue. Let us love one another, let us practice mercy and forgiveness, let us have peace, born of fellow-feeling . . .

Let my joy be of altruistic living, of doing good to others. Happiness is unto him from who happiness proceeds to any other human being.

—Zoroastrian prayer

I know
that poverty must cease.
I know this through the brokenness
and conflict in my heart.
I know
that protest is my most prophetic act
and that the world is longing
for a new soul, a new healing moment.
I know
that when we awaken to our origins
and become truly human
we bring hope to the children
and to the earth.
I feel called today
to bring the people together to break the bread
and tell the story.
I feel called today
to be a mystic in action,
aligned to the dynamics of the universe.
I feel called today
to give my gift,
to listen to the heartbeat of the broken world;
to heal the fragmentation of people and planet.
I feel called today
to celebrate the wonder of creation

and respond to sacredness and the
challenges of life.
I feel called today
to participate in the work of my time,
to fall in love,
to feel at home.
I feel called today
to be inflamed with enduring hope,
to be at one with the universe,
to be touched by God.
I feel called today
To compose a new paragraph for life.

  —James Conlon

In every child who is born under no matter what
circumstances and of no matter what parents, the
potentiality of the human race is born again, and in
him, too, once more, and each of us, our terrific
responsibility toward human life: toward the utmost
idea of goodness, of the horror of terrorism, and of
God.

  —James Agee

No statistic can express what it is to see even one child in such a way; to see a mother sitting hour after hour leaning her child's body against her own; to see the child's head turn on limbs which are unnaturally still, stiller than in sleep, to want to stop even that small movement because it is so obvious that there is so little energy left inside the child's life; . . . to see the uncomprehending panic in eyes which are still the clear and lucid eyes of a child; and then to know, in one endless moment, that life has gone.

—James P. Grant, former executive director of
 UNICEF

We look forward to the time when the power to love will replace the love of power. Then will our world know the blessings of peace.

—William Gladstone

If there is righteousness in the heart,
There will be beauty in character.
If there is beauty in character,
There will be harmony in the home.

When there is harmony in the home,
There will be order in the nation.
When there is order in the nation,
There will be peace in the world.
　　—Sri Sathya Sai Baba

How is it they live for eons in such harmony—
the billions of stars—

when most men can barely go a minute
without declaring war in their mind against some
　　one they know.

There are wars where no one marches with a flag,
though that does not keep casualties
from mounting.

Our hearts irrigate this earth.
We are fields before
each other.

How can we live in harmony?
First we need to
know

we are all madly in love
with the same
God.

> —Saint Thomas Aquinas, "We Are Fields Before
> Each Other"
> *Translated by Daniel Ladinsky*

Beyond the beliefs of any one religion, there is the
truth of the human spirit. Beyond the power of
nations, there is the power of the human heart.
Beyond the ordinary mind, the power of wisdom,
love, and healing energy are at work in the universe.
When we can find peace within our hearts, we contact these universal powers. This is our only hope.

> —Tarthang Tulku

O Most High, help to bring thy light into the dark-
ened conditions of the world! Be gracious to us thy
humble servants and bless us with illumination as to
that which is Divinely relevant to the fulfillment of
thy will!

O Most High, inspire thy servants throughout
the world to further efforts toward leading back thy
children who are led astray to the right way, and to

live and act on the faith of what has been taught by the great founders of the religions!

Bless all spiritual leaders with thy power and enable them to give help, joy, comfort, and reassurance to those suffering, to whom they minister!

—Shinto prayer

Every person alive on this planet is a creator and contributor to the transformation of our species, and each person creates this transformation by healing themselves, and by choosing differently— moment by moment, incident by incident, day by day.

—Patricia Sun

I salute you, Glorious Virgin, star more brilliant than the sun, redder than the freshest rose, whiter than any lily, higher in heaven than any of the saints. The whole earth reveres you, accept my praise and come to my aid. In the midst of your so glorious days in heaven, do not forget the miseries of this earth; turn your gaze of kindness on all those who suffer and struggle and whose lips are soaked in the bitterness of this life. Have pity on those who

loved each other and were torn apart. Have pity on
the loneliness of the heart, on the feebleness of our
faith, on the objects of our tenderness. Have pity on
those who weep, on those who pray, on those who
tremble. Give everyone hopefulness and peace.

—Ancient prayer of protection
Translated by Andrew Harvey

Discomfort of any kind also becomes the basis for
practice. We breathe in knowing that our pain is
shared; there are people all over the earth feeling
just as we do right now. This simple gesture is a
seed of compassion for self and other. If we want,
we can go further. We can wish that a specific person or all beings could be free of suffering and its
causes. In this way our toothaches, our insomnia,
our divorces, and our terror become our link with
all humanity.

—Pema Chödrön

Listen to the deeds of Kuan Yin
Responding compassionately on every side
With great vows, deep as the ocean,
Through inconceivable periods of time,

Serving innumerable Buddhas,
Giving great, clear, and pure vows . . .
To hear her name, to see her body,
To hold her in the heart, is not in vain,
For she can extinguish the suffering
    of existence.

—From the Buddhist Lotus Sutra

When you see earth from the moon, you don't see
any divisions there of nations or states. This might
be the symbol for the new mythology to come.
That is the country that we are going to be celebrating. And those are the people that we are one with.

—Joseph Campbell

We pray for the power to be gentle; the strength to
be forgiving; the patience to be understanding; and
the endurance to accept the consequences to holding to what we believe to be right.

    May we put our trust in the power of good to
overcome evil and the power of love to overcome
hatred. We pray for the vision to see and the faith
to believe in a world emancipated from violence, a
new world where fear shall no longer lead men to

commit injustice, nor selfishness make them bring suffering to others.

Help us to devote our whole life and thought and energy to the task of making peace, praying always for the inspiration and the power to fulfill the destiny for which we were created.

—Adapted prayer from Week of Prayer for World Peace, 1978

Maybe it was grace, maybe pure chance. But I started to see a new world, a system that I hadn't seen before. People were all connected, lifting one another up or tearing down. Everybody doing one or the other. The whole universe was being created and destroyed at the same time, every minute. Once I started to see that, I wanted to be one who lifted.

—Erin McGraw

Prayers for Our Planet

Grandfather,
Look at our brokenness.

We know that in all creation
Only the human family
Has strayed from the Sacred Way.

We know that we are the ones
who are divided
And we are the ones
who must come back together
to walk in the Sacred Way.

Grandfather,
Sacred One,
Teach us love, compassion, and honor

that we may heal the earth
and heal each other.
    —Ojibway people of Canada

When you see something that is broken, fix it.
When you find something that is lost, return it.
When you see something that needs to be done,
do it. In that way, you will take care of your world
and repair creation.
    —Lawrence Kushner

Justice rolls down like a river
Compassion and peace shall flow like a stream,
The hills, rocks and valleys, oceans and trees
Sing out their song: We are one.
Sing out their song: We are one.

All of creation, the Great Dance.
Only one tribe, one clan.
Dignity, peace and honor
To the earth, each woman and man.

Deep be the peace of the dark night
Brightened and blessed by the stars

Calling us now to awaken.
Gathering hearts near and far.

Surrounded by rich ancient wisdom,
Circling within and around,
Embracing the beauty in stillness,
Bursting in one Sacred Sound.

Our hopes and our dreams go before us,
Our longing to heal, to be whole,
Together we birth a new moment,
The Great Work of hands, heart and soul.

—Diane Forrest, OP, "We Are One"

We are all children of the Great Spirit, we all belong
to Mother Earth. Our planet is in great trouble and
if we keep carrying old grudges and do not work
together, we will all die.

—Chief Seattle

Out of life comes death,
and out of death, life,
Out of the young, the old,
and out of the old, the young,

Out of waking, sleep,
and out of sleep, waking,
The stream of creation and dissolution
never stop.

   —Heracleitus

Do you not see how your Lord lengthens the shadows? Had it been His will He could have made
them constant. But He makes the sun their guide;
little by little he shortens them.

   It is He who had made the night a mantle
for you and sleep a rest. He makes each day a
   resurrection.

   It is He who drives the winds as harbingers of
His mercy and sends down pure water from the sky,
so that He may give life to dead lands and quench
the thirst of man and beast.

   —The Koran

Climb the mountains and get their good tidings.
Nature's peace will flow into you as sunshine flows
into trees. The winds will blow their own freshness
into you while cares will drop off like autumn leaves.

   —John Muir

Earth teach me stillness
   as the grasses are stilled with light.
Earth teach me suffering
   as old stones suffer with memory.
Earth teach me humility
   as blossoms are humble
   with beginning.
Earth teach me caring
   as the mother who secures
   her young.
Earth teach me courage
   as the tree which stands all alone.
Earth teach me limitation
   as the ant which crawls on
   the ground.
Earth teach me freedom
   as the eagle which soars in the sky.
Earth teach me resignation
   as the leaves which die in the fall.
Earth teach me regeneration
   as the seed which rises
   in the spring.
Earth teach me to forget myself
   as melted snow forgets its life.
Earth teach me to remember kindness
   as dry fields weep with rain.
   —The Ute of North America

The love for all living creatures is the most noble
attribute of man.

—Charles Darwin

Hear our humble prayer, O God, for our friends
the animals, especially for animals who are suffering; for any that are hunted or lost or deserted or
frightened or hungry; for all that must be put to
death. We entreat for them all thy mercy and pity
and for those who deal with them we ask a heart
of compassion, gentle hands and kindly words.
Make us ourselves to be true friends to animals
and so to share the blessing of the merciful.

—Albert Schweitzer

Crush not yonder ant as it draggeth along its grain;
for it too liveth, and its life is sweet to it. A shadow
there must be, and a stone upon that heart, that
could wish to sorrow the heart even of an ant!

—Sheikh Muslih Addin Sadi

All the cattle are resting in the fields,
The trees and the plants are growing,
The birds flutter above the marshes,
Their wings uplifted in adoration,
And all the sheep are dancing,
All winged things are flying,
They live when you have shone on them.

    —Ancient Egyptian poem to the sun

A human being is a part of the whole called by us
"Universe"—a part limited in time and space. He
experiences himself, his thoughts and feelings as
something separated from the rest, a kind of optical
delusion of his consciousness. This delusion is a kind
of prison for us, restricting us to our personal desires
and to affection for a few persons nearest us. Our
task must be to free ourselves from this prison by
widening our circle of compassion to embrace all
living creatures and the whole of nature in its beauty.

    —Albert Einstein

The Lord dwells in the hearts of all creatures and
whirls them around upon the wheel of maya. Run

to him for refuge with all your strength and peace
profound will be yours through his grace.

—Bhagavad Gita

Even if I knew that tomorrow the world would go
to pieces, I would still plant my apple tree.

—Martin Luther King Jr.

The world before me
is restored in beauty.
The world behind me
is restored in beauty.
The world below me
is restored in beauty.
The world above me
is restored in beauty.
All things around me
are restored in beauty.
It is finished in beauty.
It is finished in beauty.
It is finished in beauty.
It is finished in beauty.
It is finished in beauty.

—Native American prayer

We can create a world as yet unimagined, a world undreamed, yet dimly felt. We are like the corn. Mysteriously hidden within each of us are the seeds that can germinate into a new society, a new planet. Like the corn, we have hidden deep within our living process a wisdom that reaches back to all knowledge and beyond to all possibilities. Our very existence is potential. Potential is always that which is, as yet, unexpressed. We have the wisdom of the ancestors reaching back to the mighty power of all creation . . . within us.

—Ann Wilson Schaef

I love to think of nature as an unlimited broadcasting station through which God speaks to us every hour, if we will only tune in.

—George Washington Carver

There is a squirrel napping in the sun.
There is a squirrel napping in the plum.
Plump and plain as day for all to see,
Poets, children, hawks, the neighbors, me,

Stretched out lithe on limb,
Paws extended out akimbo,
Tail hung low for ballast,
Eyes, squirrel-bright and wide,
Slowly falling shut.
Nut-brown, deeply furry in plum blossoms,
Sleeping in cat-like regal calm,
In fact, with almost panther-like aplomb.

Makes one reconsider squirrels.
Didn't know they napped.
Thought they only skittered and ate.
Thought that they were always late.
Thought that victimhood was their natural fate—
Cute and harried,
Beware-ied.

Wait!
If a squirrel can be safe,
And even cavalier,
Can a woman then
Live without fear?

Who knows?
It is enough to see a squirrel so
For just a moment, just a thought,
Just to know that all I think I know,
Is not necessarily all so.

    —Ann Kyle-Brown, "The Squirrel I"

The inhabitant or soul of the universe is never seen; its voice alone is heard. . . . It has a gentle voice like a woman, a voice so fine and gentle that even children cannot become afraid. What it says is, "Be not afraid of the universe."

—Alaskan saying

Our words have been spoken, our wisdom
    exchanged;
And questions arise that cannot be tamed.
We inhabit a mys'try that's deep and profound.
The arc of creation rests on holy ground.

So rest now the words while the echoes endure
And come home to the silence where wisdom is pure.
And wait in the shadows with light seeping through.
Yes, wait on the Spirit, the source of the new!

In silence, the chaos can be held afresh;
Even in those times when the Spirit is crushed.
And the flickering wick can be fanned into flame.
While the Spirit of silence re-echoes our name.
Amen.

—Diarmuid O'Murchu, "Call to Silence"

He who is in the sun, and in the fire and in the heart of man is One. He who knows this is one with the One.

   —The Upanishads

Quick to judge
Tempted by drink
so many drugs
A prayer for Spirit's link

Our loving planet provides
Everything we need
consumerism has died—
it was courting greed

Easy to distrust
charmed by things
We'll not turn to dust
wearing diamond rings

Hearts open wide
to All that prevails
We'll flow with the tide
on God's ship of sails

We pray for Wisdom to take care
of every blade of grass
common or rare
for Spirit lasts, spirit lasts

For the alcoholic
with the golden heart
we pray for freedom from judgment
a fresh start

Due to returned cancer
that has interrupted ability
we pray for the dancer
and our own humility

For the sacrifice of plants,
animals and fish
We welcome nourishment
to Gaia's dish

For the kindnesses of strangers
in Life's many streets
Love is safety—not a danger
to the Universal beat
                —Georgia Otterson

If you're going to care about the fall of the sparrow
you can't pick and choose who's going to be the
sparrow. It's everybody.

    —Madeleine L'Engle

Once a man came to me and spoke for hours about
"His great visions of God" he felt he was having.

He asked me for confirmation, saying,
"Are these wondrous dreams true?"

I replied, "How many goats do you have?"

He looked surprised and said,
"I am speaking of sublime visions
And you ask
About goats!"

And I spoke again saying,
"Yes, brother—how many do you have?"

"Well, Hafiz, I have sixty-two."

"And how many wives?"
Again he looked surprised, then said,
"Four."

"How many rose bushes in your garden,
How many children,
Are your parents still alive,
Do you feed the birds in winter?"

And to all he answered.

Then I said,
"You asked me if I thought your visions were true,
I would say that they were if they make you become
More human,

More kind to every creature and plant
That you know."

    —Hafiz, "Becoming Human"
     Translated by Daniel Ladinsky

I sing for the animals,
Out of the earth I sing for them.
A Horse nation
I sing for them.
Out of the earth
I sing for them,
The animals
I sing for them.

    —Teton Sioux

If thy heart were right, then every creature would be
a mirror of life and a book of holy doctrine.
   —Thomas à Kempis

In the rain
Everything is touched
Whether it will or not,
Likes or dislikes.

Its clarity
Reflects everything—
Bends all the light
Through its dropped lens

Catches the sun
In points
Which depend from branch or stem

It runs along
On everything
And cleans
Gleans
Glistens and

Wrinkled . . . in streams
It gleams

Colored transparent
It has no viewpoint
Or every viewpoint
It has no location
Or every location

In the rain
We are all wet
No blessings are withheld
None are excepted from its care
Anyone can enjoy its freedom
To give
Everything to everyone
Endlessly providing
The wonder and grace of love!
 —Daniel Brady, "In the Rain"

Keep a green tree in your heart
and perhaps a singing bird
will come.
 —Chinese proverb

How wonderful, O Lord, are the works of Your
    hands!
The heavens declare Your glory;
The arch of sky displays Your handiwork.
In Your love You have given us the power
To behold the beauty of Your world
Robed in all its splendor.

The sun and stars, the valleys and hills,
The rivers and lakes all disclose Your presence.
The roaring breakers of the sea tell of Your awesome
    might;
The beasts of the field and the birds of the air
Bespeak Your wondrous will.

In Your goodness, You have made us able to hear
The music of the world. The voices of loved ones
Reveal to us that You are in our midst.
A divine voice sings through all creation.
    —Author unknown

Whoever is kind to the creatures of God is kind to
himself.
    —Mohammad

How can we face the pain and the plight of those
who live in the dark?
How can we open the locks that are tied round
many a mind and a heart?
How can we liberate people in hope for the new
day that dawns on us all?
The answer my friend, is blowing in the wind, the
answer is blowing in the wind!

While parliamentarians fail to inspire and financiers
convolute;
And the powers from on high are so blind and confused—even Church folk can't recognise truth!
While systems collapse and things fall apart, a new
birth emerges elsewhere.
The future, my friend, is blowing in the wind, the
future is blowing . . .

Let's listen instead to the margins crying out, the
voices for too long subdued.
Let's listen instead to our Planet, the Earth, whose
story we oft misconstrued.
The wisdom of women ignored and repressed, is
haunting our world anew.
So, new hope, my friend, is blowing in the wind,
new hope is blowing . . .

How can we reclaim a faith to sustain the prophets
    that open new ways?
And can we discern the disturbing voice of the
    Spirit who now recreates?
We need a new heart and a mind open wide—
    receptive to this hour of grace.
Just listen, my friend, to the vibrating wind, the
    answer is blowing . . .

The Spirit that broods at creation's first dawn,
    unravelling the chaos of life,
Continues to breathe in the birthing and dying, in
    the longing, the struggle and strife.
For God's sake don't tie down the Spirit that blows,
    reweaving the rhythms of time.
We're called to befriend what's blowing in the wind,
    the Spirit who blows in . . .

    —Diarmuid O'Murchu, "The Spirit Who
    Blows . . . "

A camellia
Dropped down into still waters
Of a deep dark well
    —Buson

O merciful Father, who has given life to many and
lovest all that Thou has made, give us the spirit of
Thine own loving kindness that we may show
mercy to all helpless creatures. Especially would we
pray for those which minister to our comfort, that
they may be treated with tenderness of hands, in
thankfulness of heart, and that we may discover
Thee, the Creator, in all created things. Amen.

—Author unknown

If you put your hands on this oar with me,
they will never harm another, and they will come
    to find
they hold everything you want.

If you put your hands on this oar with me, they
    would no longer
lift anything to your
mouth that might wound your precious land—
that sacred earth that is
your body.

If you put your soul against this oar with me,
the power that made the universe will enter your
    sinew

from a source not outside your limbs, but from a
    holy realm
that lives in us.

Exuberant is existence, time a husk.
When the moment cracks open, ecstasy leaps out
    and devours space;
love goes mad with the blessings, like my words give.

Why lay yourself on the torturer's rack of the past
    and future?
The mind that tries to shape tomorrow beyond its
    capacities
will find no rest.

Be kind to yourself, dear—to our innocent follies.
Forget any sounds or touch you knew that did not
    help you dance.
You will come to see that all evolves us.

If you put your heart against the earth with me, in
    serving
every creature, our Beloved will enter you from our
    sacred realm
and we will be, we will be
so happy.

    —Rumi, "That Lives in Us"
    Translated by Daniel Ladinsky

We have forgotten how to be good guests, how to
walk lightly on the earth as its other creatures do.
　　—Stockholm Conference, 1972

We return thanks to our mother,
　　the earth, which sustains us.
We return thanks to the rivers and streams,
　　which supply us with water.
We return thanks to all herbs,
　　which furnish medicines for the cure to our
　　　　diseases.
We return thanks to the corn, and to her sisters,
　　the beans and squashes,
　　which give us life.
We return thanks to the bushes and trees,
　　which provide us with fruit.
We return thanks to the wind,
　　which, moving in the air, has banished diseases.
We return thanks to the moon and stars,
　　which have given to us their light
　　when the sun was gone.
We return thanks to our grandfather He-no,
　　that he has protected his grandchildren
　　from witches and reptiles,
　　and has given to us his rain.

We return thanks to the sun,
    that he has looked upon the earth
    with a beneficent eye.
Lastly, we return thanks to the Great Spirit,
    in whom is embodied all goodness,
    and who directs all things
    for the good of his children.
    —Iroquois prayer

Praised are You, Adonai our God, Guide of the
Universe, who creates innumerable living beings
and their needs, for all the things You have created
to sustain every living being. Praised are You, the
life of the Universe.
    —Jewish blessing

When I was the stream, when I was the
forest, when I was still the field,
when I was every hoof, foot
fin and wing, when I
was the sky
itself,

no one ever asked me did I have a purpose, no
    one ever

wondered was there anything I might need,
for there was nothing
I could not
love.

It was when I left all we once were that
the agony began, the fear and questions came;
and I wept; I wept. And tears
I had never known
before.

So I returned to the river, I returned to
the mountains. I asked for their hand in marriage
   again,
I begged—I begged to wed every object
and creature.

And when they accepted,
God was ever present in my arms.
And He did not say,
"Where have you
been?"

For then I knew my soul—every soul—
has always held
Him.

> —Meister Eckhart, "When I Was the Forest"
> *Translated by Daniel Ladinsky*

There is no form without the gift of the Mother
and the Father. From Father Sky comes your consciousness and Mother Earth is your very bones.
To sense the balance of the Mother/Father, Father/
Mother within one's own being, one's own nature,
is a way to renew the Earth, to renew our hearts, to
renew the vision.

    —Dhyani Ywahoo

We seek your forgiveness
for our indifference to the numerous signs
of your presence around us,
for our inability to value the skies and the earth
as our only home,
for our inability to make the connections
between our lives and the earth
from where we emerge and to which we shall
    proceed.
We pray for a profound change
in the hearts of all men and women
so that we may stop the destruction
of the ecological balance,
the pollution of our skies and water,
the decimation of our forests

and the accompanying impoverishment
of the human spirit.
Our Lord, You have not created this world in vain.

—Unitarian Universalist Prayer

There is a certain consideration, and a general duty
of humanity, that binds us not only to the animals,
which have life and feeling, but even to the trees
and plants. We owe justice to me, and kindness and
benevolence to all other creatures who may be sus-
ceptible of it. There is some intercourse between
them and us, and some mutual obligation.

—Michel de Montaigne

May all beings have happiness and the causes of
    happiness;
    this is immeasurable loving kindness;
May all beings be liberated from suffering and the
    causes of suffering;
    this is immeasurable compassion;
May all beings be free of suffering and always stay
        happy;
    this is immeasurable joy;
May all beings be free of grasping and aversion
    toward others,

and develop faith in the equality of all beings;
   this is immeasurable equanimity.
   —The Four Immeasurable Vows, Tantric Buddhism

If only we know, boss, what the stones and rain and flowers say. Maybe they call—call us—and we don't hear them. When will people's ears open, boss? When shall we have our eyes open to see? When shall we open our arms to embrace everything—stones, rain, flowers, and men?
   —Nikos Kazantzakis

This earth is a garden, the Lord its gardener, cherishing all, none neglected.
   —Sikh blessing

This we know: The Earth does not belong to man, man belongs to the Earth. All things are connected like the blood that unites us all: Man did not weave the web of life, he is but a strand in it. Whatever he does to the web he does to himself.
   —Chief Seattle

It is only logical that the pauperization of our soul and the soul of society coincide with the pauperization of the environment. One is the cause and the reflection of the other.

—Paolo Soleri

Black cloudbank broken
Scatters in the night . . . now see
Moon-lighted mountains!

—Basho

If I spent enough time with the tiniest creature—even a caterpillar—I would never have to prepare a sermon. So full of God is every creature.

—Meister Eckhart

I have noticed in my life that all men have a liking for some special animal, tree, plant, or spot of earth. If men would pay more attention to those preferences and seek what is best to do in order to make

themselves worthy of that toward which they are
so attracted, they might have dreams which would
purify their lives. Let a man decide upon his favorite and make a study of it, learning its innocent
ways. Let him learn to understand its sounds and
motions. The animals want to communicate with
man, but Wakan'tanka does not intend that they
shall do so directly—man must do the greater part
in securing an understanding.

    —Sioux

Until one has loved an animal, a part of one's soul
remains unawakened.

    —Anatole France

And the stars down so close, and sadness and pleasure so close together, really the same thing. . . .
The stars are close and dear and I have joined the
brotherhood of the worlds. And everything's holy—
everything, even me.

    —John Steinbeck

Deep peace of the running waves to you,
Deep peace of the flowing air to you,
Deep peace of the quiet earth to you,
Deep peace of the shining stars to you,
Deep peace of the shades of night to you,
Moon and stars always giving light to you.

—Gaelic blessing

We recognize the spiritual in all creation, and
believe that we draw power from it.

—Ohiyesa, Dakota Sioux

At Tara today in this fateful hour
I place all heaven with its power,
And the sun with its brightness,
And the snow with its whiteness,
And fire with all the strength it has,
And lightning with its rapid wrath
And the winds with their swiftness along the path,
And the sea with its deepness,
And the rocks with their steepness
And the Earth with its starkness,
All these I place

By God's almighty help and grace,
Between myself and the powers of Darkness.
   —Saint Patrick

One flower at a time. I want to hear what it
    is saying.
   —Robert Francis

The little cares that fretted me,
    I lost them yesterday
Among the fields above the sea,
    Among the winds at play;
Among the lowing of the herds,
    The rustling of the trees,
Among the singing of the birds,
    The humming of the bees.

The foolish fears of what may pass,
    I cast them all away
Among the clover-scented grass,
    Among the new-mown hay;
Among the hushing of the corn
    Where drowsy poppies nod,

Where ill thoughts die and good are born,
    Out in the fields with God.
    —Author unknown

The poetry of earth is never dead.
    —John Keats

Over the winter glaciers
I see the summer glow;
And through the wild-piled snowdrift
The warm rosebuds below.
    —Ralph Waldo Emerson

Every blade of grass, each leaf, each separate floret
and petal, is an inscription speaking of hope.
    —Richard Jeffries

Wisdom, O holy Word of God, you govern all creation with your strong yet tender care. Come and
show your people the way to salvation.
    —Advent Antiphon, Liturgy of the Hours

Lord, may we love all Your creation, including all the earth and every grain of sand in it. May we love every leaf, every ray of Your light.

May we love the animals: you have given them the rudiments of thought and joy untroubled. Let us not trouble it; let us not harass them, let us not deprive them of their happiness, let us not work against your intent.

For we acknowledge unto You that all is like an ocean, all is flowing and blending, and that to withhold any measure of love from anything in Your universe is to withhold the same measure from You.

—Adapted from a passage by Fyodor Dostoevsky

The Lord of the universe is more splendid than the sun and the stars. He will never leave me!

—Saint Agnes

Praised be you, my Lord, through our Sister Mother Earth, who sustains us, governs us, and who produces varied fruits with colored flowers and herbs.

Praised be you, my Lord, through Brother Wind and through the air, cloudy and serene, and every kind of weather.

Praised be you, my Lord, through Sister Moon and the stars in heaven; you formed them clear and precious and beautiful.

Praised be you, my Lord, through Brother Fire, through whom you light the night and he is beautiful and playful and robust and strong.

Praised be you, my Lord, with all your creatures, especially Sir Brother Sun, who is the day and through whom you give us light. And he is beautiful and radiant with great splendors and bears likeness of You, Most High One.

—Saint Francis of Assisi

Surely God means nature to sensitize us to other silences and rhythms. . . . All nature is a sign of the sacred in our midst.

—Meinrad Craighead

When I walk through thy woods,
may my right foot and my left foot

be harmless to the little creatures
that move in its grasses: as it is said
by the mouth of thy prophet,
They shall not hurt nor destroy
in all my holy mountain.

    —Rabbi Moshe Hakotun

I was seeing in a sacred manner
the shapes of all things
in the spirit,
and the shape of all shapes
as they must live together
like one being.
And I saw that the sacred hoop
of my people was one of many hoops
that made one circle,
wide as daylight and as starlight,
and in the center
grew one mighty flowering tree
to shelter all the children
of one mother and one father.
And I saw that it was holy.

    —Black Elk

We are an immeasurable speck in the immense galaxies. Yet we are part of a divine creativity. . . . To sense the awesome presence of God in this world is to gain insight into who we are, where we belong, to find our place in the scheme of things.

—Sharon Blessum Sawatzky

A short summer night . . .
But in this solemn darkness
One peony bloomed

—Buson

I am the one whose praise echoes on high
I adorn all the earth
I am the breeze that nurtures all things green
I encourage blossoms to flourish with ripening
    fruits.
I am led by the spirit to feed the purest streams.
I am the rain coming from the dew
That causes the grasses to laugh with the joy of life.
I am the yearning for good.

—Hildegard of Bingen

If we ground ourselves in the future, rather than in history, decidedly imagining a vital future that includes the natural world and all of us, the task becomes easier. We see the future in our mind's heart and we take the small next step that will enable us to get there together. This is the activity of radical hope.

—Deena Metzger

Blessed are the hopeful, they hold a promise of
    tomorrow.
Blessed are the courageous, they embrace the
    challenge of today.
Blessed are the forgiving, they are free of the burden
    of the past.
Blessed are the people of prolonged engagement,
    they will create a better world for the children.
Blessed are the disappointed, they will rise and
    anticipate a better day.
Blessed are the self-forgetful, they will engage in a
    compassionate embrace.
Blessed are the flowers, bursting forth in the spring.
Blessed are the children, celebrating spontaneity and
    new life.

Blessed are the contemplatives, they will embrace
the universe as one.

Blessed are the liberators, they will set all the
captives free.

Blessed are the creation-centered people, they will
appreciate the beauty of the earth.

Blessed are the engaged mystics, they will ignite a
fire on the earth and unite the stars and the
street.

—James Conlon, "Beatitudes for the New
Creation"

The fundamental spiritual reality of the Universe is
that it is pervaded with Love and Goodness. We are
to be witness to that possibility, to be partners with
God in the healing and transformation of the world.

—Michael Lerner

Each one of us is responsible for how the universe
will unfold.

—David A. Cooper

Resources and Recommended Reading

The following is a list of resources that you may find helpful for further reflection and study:

BOOKS

Artichoke Heart: Journey through Loss to Rediscover the Soul and Celebrate Living, by Helen Elaine (Hara Publishing, 2000).

Earth Prayers from Around the World: 365 Prayers, Poems and Invocations for Honoring the Earth, edited by Elizabeth Roberts and Elias Amidon (HarperSanFrancisco, 1991).

The Gentle Weapon: Prayers for Everyday and Not-So-Everyday Moments (Rebbe Nachman of Breslov), adapted by Moshe Mykoff and S. C. Mizrahi with the Breslov Research Institute (Jewish Lights Publishing, 2000).

Gifts of Suffering: A Chaplain's First Year, by Judy Tretheway (booklet published by the author, 2000; *judyt@ accessbee.com*).

Good Poems for Hard Times, edited by Garrison Keillor (Viking Penguin, 2005).

One God, Shared Hope: Twenty Threads Shared by Judaism, Christianity, and Islam, by Maggie Oman Shannon (Red Wheel/Weiser, 2003).

Poems to Live By in Troubling Times, edited by Joan Murray (Beacon Press, 2006).

Prayers at 3 A.M.: Poems, Songs, Chants and Prayers for the Middle of the Night, edited by Phil Cousineau (Conari Press, 1995).

Prayers for Comfort in Difficult Times, by Marguerite Guzman Bouvard (Wind Publications, 2004).

Prayers for Healing: 365 Blessings, Poems, and Meditations from Around the World, edited by Maggie Oman (Conari Press, 1997).

Prayers for a Thousand Years: Inspiration from Leaders and Visionaries Around the World, edited by Elizabeth Roberts and Elias Amidon (HarperSanFrancisco, 1999).

Praying through Poetry: Hope for Violent Times, by Peggy Rosanthal (St. Anthony Messenger Press, 2003).

Psalms for Troubled Times: Prayers of Hope and Challenge, by Barbara Gibson (Crestline Press, 2003).

Rilke on Love and Other Difficulties: Translations and Considerations of Rainer Maria Rilke, by John J. L. Mood (W. W. Norton & Company, 1975).

Simple Prayers and Blessings: Inspirations for the New Millennium, by Gary Wilde and Margaret Anne Huffman (Publications International Ltd., 1999).

A String and a Prayer: How to Make and Use Personal Prayer Beads, by Eleanor Wiley and Maggie Oman Shannon (Red Wheel/Weiser, 2002).

Talking to God: Personal Prayers for Times of Joy, Sadness, Struggle and Celebration, by Naomi Levy (Alfred A. Knopf, 2002).

The 12 Step Prayer Book: A Collection of Favorite 12 Step Prayers and Inspirational Readings, written and compiled by Bill P. and Lisa D. (Hazelden Foundation, 2004).

A Way Forward: Spiritual Guidance for Our Troubled Times,
    by Anna Voight and Nevil Drury (Red Wheel/Weiser,
    2003).
The Way We Pray: Prayer Practices from Around the World, by
    Maggie Oman Shannon (Conari Press, 2001).
"With God All Things Are Possible!": A Handbook of Life by
    Life-Study Fellowship (Bantam Books, 1974).

WEBSITES

www.beliefnet.com
An online magazine focusing on inspiration, spirituality,
and faith.

www.explorefaith.org
Offering "spiritual guidance for anyone seeking a path to
God."

www.karlanthony.com
The website of singer-songwriter Karl Anthony, which contains links to songs included in this anthology.

www.newdimensions.org
The website of New Dimensions Radio, "changing the
world, one broadcast at a time."

www.prayerforce.org
One person's website devoted to prayers for challenges
around the world.

www.riverprayers.org
The website of Ann Keeler Evans, containing prayers for all
circumstances of life.

www.spiritualityandpractice.com
The resource-rich website of authors Frederic and Mary
Ann Brussat.

www.unityonline.org
Unity's online prayer and publishing outreach.

www.worldprayers.org
An interfaith, online collection of prayers from around the
world.

ORGANIZATIONS AND
STUDY OPPORTUNITIES

Angeles Arrien Foundation for Cross-Cultural Education
    and Research
www.angelesarrien.com

Bread for the Journey
www.breadforthejourney.org

Institute of Noetic Sciences
www.ions.org

Sophia Center at Holy Names University
www.hnu.edu/sophia

The New Story
www.thenewstory.com

MAGAZINES AND NEWSLETTERS

Daily Word
www.unityonline.org

"The Monastic Way"
www.benetvision.org

Ode
www.odemagazine.com

Sacred Journey
www.sacredjourney.org

Science of Mind
www.scienceofmind.com

Sojourners
www.sojo.net

Spirituality and Health
www.spiritualityhealth.org

Yes!
www.yesmagazine.com

Acknowledgments

First on the list of the many people to thank is Brenda Knight, whose inspired idea was the genesis of *Prayers for Hope and Comfort.* Many thanks also to Jan Johnson, Rachel Leach, and all the other wonderful people at Conari Press who worked so hard to make this book a balm for the senses as well as the soul.

Thanks to Diane Berke, Daniel Brady, Kathryn Brenson, Catherine Cameron, Donna Chan, Deborah Clark, Ann Keeler Evans, Diane Forrest, Vadette Goulet, Margaret Jain, Ann Kyle-Brown, Judith McWalter-Sante, Magdolene Mogyorosi, Georgia Otterson, Mary Peterson, Desiree Sangeetha, Molly Starr, Judy Tretheway, Wendy Wolters, and Pamela Ayo Yetunde for their original contributions; and to Diane Berke, Bea Boxley, Jane Burruss, Sheryl Cotleur, Connie Cross, Lee Gaillard, Vadette Goulet, Nina Ham, Geneva Kelly, Aida Merriweather, Judy Ranieri, Jamie Walters, and Wendy Wolters for their suggestions. Additional gratitude goes to Karl Anthony, Angeles Arrien, Mary Ann Brussat, Phil

Cousineau, Janice Farrell, Tom Grady, and Persephone Zill for their various forms of help to further this project. And many thanks to Jim Conlon and Sarah Stockton, who read the first draft of this book and made insightful comments that have enriched the final product.

On a personal note, thanks and love to my mother, Mary Jane Oman; my brother, Carl Oman; and the memory of my father, Frederick Oman. Heartfelt appreciation to Kathryn Brenson and MaryEllen Jirak for their kindness when times felt really hard. Most important, deep love and gratitude to my family—this book could not have been created if it weren't for the loving help and support of my husband, Scott Shannon, who spent many evenings and weekends with our daughter as I worked on this book; and to the light of our lives, Chloe Shannon, for so graciously understanding when Mommy needed to go down to her office to work . . . again.

Finally, I thank God for the opportunity and privilege of shepherding *Prayers for Hope and Comfort* into being. I am deeply blessed, and so grateful.

Index of First Lines

"Come Holy Spirit, breathe down upon our troubled world" 194

"Come, Lord, and cover me with the night" 27

"Creative force, creating still, thank you for my beloved [pet's name]" 90

"Crush not yonder ant as it draggeth along its grain . . ." 245

"Cultures develop from the integrity of the innumerable lived details . . ." 167

"Darkness cannot drive out darkness: only love can do that" 78

"Dead my fine old hopes" 38

"Dear God, guide me to always have trust in you" 69

"Dear Lord, Creator of the world, help us love one another . . ." 223

"Deep peace of the running waves to you . . ." 270

"Discomfort of any kind also becomes the basis for practice" 237

"Divine Spirit, please guide us that we may do here" 106

"Do all the good you can . . ." 140

"Do not believe that all greatness and heroism are in the past" 170

"Do not look forward to the changes and chances of this life in fear . . ." 68

"Do not stand by my grave and weep" 103

"Do the thing . . ." 150

"Do what you can . . ." 167

"Do you not see how your Lord lengthens the shadows?" 243

"Don't look for the flaws as you go through life" 131

Permissions

Thanks to the following authors for their original contributions to *Prayers for Hope and Comfort:* Diane Berke, Daniel Brady, Kathryn Brenson, Catherine Cameron, Donna Chan, Deborah Clark, Ann Keeler Evans, Diane Forrest, Vadette Goulet, Margaret Jain, Ann Kyle-Brown, Judith McWalter-Sante, Magdolene Mogyorosi, Georgia Otterson, Mary Peterson, Desiree Sangeetha, Molly Starr, Judy Tretheway, Wendy Wolters, and Pamela Ayo Yetunde.

Thanks for permission to excerpt from the following previously published works:

Permissions

An exhaustive effort has been made to clear all reprint permissions for this book. This process has been complicated;
if any required acknowledgments have been omitted, it is
unintentional. If notified, the publisher will be pleased to
rectify any omission in future editions.

About the Author

Maggie Oman Shannon is the author of *Prayers for Healing; The Way We Pray; One God, Shared Hope: Twenty Threads Shared by Judaism, Christianity, and Islam;* and coauthor of *A String and a Prayer: How to Make and Use Prayer Beads.* A spiritual director, workshop leader, and retreat facilitator, Oman Shannon is the founder of The New Story (*www.thenewstory.com*), a coaching and consulting business focused on helping people create deeper meaning in their lives. She lives in San Francisco with her husband and daughter.

To Our Readers

Conari Press, an imprint of Red Wheel/Weiser, publishes books on topics ranging from spirituality, personal growth, and relationships to women's issues, parenting, and social issues. Our mission is to publish quality books that will make a difference in people's lives—how we feel about ourselves and how we relate to one another. We value integrity, compassion, and receptivity, both in the books we publish and in the way we do business.

Our readers are our most important resource, and we value your input, suggestions, and ideas about what you would like to see published. Please feel free to contact us, to request our latest book catalog, or to be added to our mailing list.

Conari Press
An imprint of Red Wheel/Weiser, LLC
500 Third Street, Suite 230
San Francisco, CA 94107
www.redwheelweiser.com